SENTO AT SIXTH AND MAIN

Preserving Landmarks of Japanese American Heritage

SENTO AT SIXTH AND MAIN

Preserving Landmarks of Japanese American Heritage

By Gail Dubrow with Donna Graves | Design by Karen Cheng

Published by the Seattle Arts Commission

Published by the Seattle Arts Commission.

Distributed by the University of Washington Press.
P.O. Box 50096 Seattle, Washington 98145-5096
www.washington.edu/uwpress

Authors
Gail Dubrow with Donna Graves

Contributors
Coll-Peter Thrush and Eugenia Woo

Designer
Karen Cheng

Library of Congress Control No. 2002101982
ISBN 0-295-98245-4 [Paper]
ISBN 0-295-98263-2 [Cloth]

This book was made possible through the generous support of the Seattle City Light Percent for Art Funds, administered by the Seattle Arts Commission, the Graham Foundation for Advanced Studies in the Fine Arts, the Simpson Center for the Humanities at the University of Washington, the Harry Bridges Center for Labor Studies at the University of Washington, and the Motoda Foundation.

CONTENTS

INTRODUCTION

Sixth and South Main is located at the margins of most maps of Seattle's downtown. But it was the center of the universe for Japanese immigrants and their American-born children who had made Shiatoru, as they called it, their home before World War II. Nothing formally marks this intersection as the historic center of Seattle's Nihonmachi (Japantown). However, older members of the community, who lived in the city before the war, recognize its historical significance.

The sento, known from the 1910s on as Hashidate-Yu, is located in the basement of the Panama Hotel, which anchors one corner of Sixth and South Main Street. Although it survives as a rare, intact example of a Japanese American public bathhouse, many similar facilities once existed in western Nihonmachi. Surveyors overlooked the surviving example in the Panama Hotel's basement when the National Register nomination for the Chinatown/International District originally was prepared as a result of their reliance on so-called windshield survey methods, which concentrated on what could be seen from the street. Fortunately, the sento's out-of-the-way location indirectly contributed to its preservation and it has benefited from responsible stewardship over the years. It survives as a real and symbolic example of the riches that await discovery by those who seek out the tangible remains of Japanese American heritage.

The Japanese phrase "barabara ni naru" means to be scattered or disassembled. Depending on the context, it can suggest the sense of loss that stems from being separated from one another or the damaged state of being broken into pieces. Certainly it is an apt phrase for describing the historical condition of the Nikkei (people of Japanese ancestry in America or overseas Japanese), who left their home prefectures for temporary work or permanent settlement in the Hawaiian Islands and along the west coast of the continental United States.

As part of the settlement process, Japanese immigrants gathered and then organized to meet their own basic needs as well as to enact traditional cultural practices. Whether building sento or erecting new community halls, immigrants reestablished and adapted Nihonjin (Japanese) practices in their new homes in western lumber camps, on valley farms, in small towns, and on the streets of major cities. Directories produced by vernacular newspapers suggest the vitality of western Nihonmachi as early as 1915, serving bachelors and those who had left families behind in the home country. Two decades later, directories from the mid-1930s swelled with listings for a wide range of community institutions that served a growing population of Japanese American families, including the Nisei (second generation Japanese Americans).

While the history of Japanese Americans is better understood with each passing year, due to a surge in scholarly research as well as community-based activity, places significant in Japanese American heritage have not yet been adequately documented, interpreted, or preserved. This book calls attention to ten places significant in Japanese American heritage on the West Coast in the hope of stimulating public support to protect the remaining landmarks.

Seattle is not the only place where the tangible remains of Japanese American heritage have vanished over time or been rendered nearly invisible. Just south of Seattle, the once-vibrant fabric of Tacoma's Nihonmachi never recovered from the forced evacuation of its Japanese and Japanese American residents during World War II. Half a century after the war's end, what little remains of the historic fabric of Tacoma's Nihonmachi continues to unravel. The last traces of it survive in the form of isolated buildings. The Whitney Memorial United Methodist Church, a Japanese American congregation, recently sold its historic property to the University of Washington, which has established a branch campus in Tacoma. The long-vacant Japanese Language School, also owned by the University, is threatened with demolition. Only the Buddhist Temple continues in its historic location. Otherwise little remains of the multi-block area that once constituted the city's Nihonmachi.

Active efforts to improve the protection of California's multicultural heritage during the 1980s, and Washington's Asian American heritage during the 1990s, resulted in the listing of numerous places associated with Japanese Americans in state and local inventories of historic properties. The places chosen for inclusion in this book are exceptionally good examples of vernacular resource types that figured prominently in many other Japanese American communities. While each of the places chosen for inclusion in this book has a unique story that merits attention, together, they also represent larger groups of cultural resources that deserve greater protection. They include lumber camps, farms, general stores, bathhouses, community halls, language schools, hospitals and midwiferies, temples, and recreational facilities such as bowling alleys. These examples only hint at the architectural heritage of Japanese America. Before many more aspects of this heritage are lost, it is important to document the surviving landmarks, plan for their protection, and develop programs of public interpretation.

Unlike the African Diaspora, which largely took place under conditions of forced migration and involuntary servitude, Japanese migration throughout the Pacific Rim was voluntary in character. Japanese immigrants to America, however, received a less than welcoming reception. Economic opportunities were colored by race, and the experience of Asian immigrants included discrimination, segregation, dispossession, and even violence. As a result, there was a darker side to the Japanese Diaspora in the form of immigration restrictions, prohibitions against property ownership, and coerced assimilation. During World War II it included the forced removal and incarceration of people of Japanese descent, including American citizens, from California, the coastal areas of Washington and Oregon, and the southern part of Arizona. These dislocations, as much as any other factor, explain the diasporic quality of Japanese American heritage.

Japanese American heritage was scattered after the swift arrest and detention of community leaders following the Japanese bombing of Pearl Harbor on December 7, 1941. Few family photograph albums survived the war as the result of thousands of individual decisions to hide and destroy mementos, such as images of relatives in the Japanese Navy. Immigrants of Japanese descent feared that government agents would misinterpret these things as signs of loyalty to the Japanese emperor. With the FBI's immediate closure of language schools, dedication to learning Japanese culture — always suspect since Japanese immigrants were considered to be "unassimilable aliens" — instantly was re-stigmatized. These attachments were taken as evidence of a suspect category of American citizenship that was used to justify wartime incarceration.

Longstanding cultural icons gained new and problematic meanings with the rise of Nazism, as the swastika, an ancient Buddhist symbol, was appropriated as the icon of National Socialism, albeit in reversed form. After the United States declared war against Japan, Buddhists concealed the symbol or removed it from their temples to protect the Nikkei community from those who confused it with loyalty to the Axis powers. The internment itself resulted in a physical and cultural Diaspora, as the material culture of Japanese America was suppressed, destroyed, scattered. The people and their culture essentially were forced into internal exile. The closure of community institutions such as dojo, temples, and language schools, and ultimately the wholesale evacuation of Japanese American communities, disassembled Japanese American heritage and unjustly deprived innocent people of their freedom.

The 1980s redress campaign began the process of healing a wound in the body politic that still requires careful tending. President Ronald Reagan signed the Civil Liberties Act in 1988. The public apology issued by the Executive branch of the federal government under President George H.W. Bush in 1990, which accompanied payments to survivors of the internment, was the most direct form of redress for the harm inflicted on those forcibly removed from their homes inside designated military areas. In recent years, the redress movement also has prompted a long overdue wave of historical revisionism, changing public perceptions of the internment from the official interpretation advanced by the federal government, which rationalized the internment as "military necessity," to the survivors' view that it represented an unjust abrogation of civil liberties.

The movement for redress has found cultural expression in the realm of public commemoration as myriad oral history projects, exhibitions, monuments, parks and memorials have been dedicated to revisiting the internment from the standpoint of Japanese Americans. In Seattle, the 50-year anniversary of Executive Order 9066 prompted a trail-blazing exhibition at the Wing Luke Asian Museum in 1992. In California, the Manzanar Committee, a tireless advocate for the preservation and interpretation of the Owens Valley internment camp, successfully built momentum for listing Manzanar as a California State Historic Landmark in 1972, paving the way for its designation as a National Historic Site two decades later. Although little remains at the sites of internment camps such as Manzanar and Minidoka, they serve as touchstones for difficult memories. Former internees have made them sites of pilgrimage. They also serve as historic sites of conscience for the American people, their presence asserting a shared commitment to facing our collective legacy of racial injustice. These additions to the National Park System represent an opportunity to weave the loose thread of Japanese American history back into the fabric of public memory.

Ironically, an unintended consequence of the campaign for redress is that World War II internment camps constitute the largest group of landmarks listed in the National Register of Historic Places that are associated with Japanese Americans. While the preservation and interpretation of the internment camps are important priorities, sustained efforts are needed to protect the full range of places that are significant in Japanese American heritage. After all, even the obvious emotional power of a visit to an internment camp is diminished for lack of knowing the scope, complexity, and character of the world the Nikkei had made.

The places highlighted in this book clearly document the imprint of Japanese immigrants and their children on the American landscape. Preservation of these landmarks, however, is complicated by their location on contested terrain, beginning with prohibitions against alien land ownership and culminating in their presence within designated military areas. With only a few exceptions, the sites covered in this book were affected by the long series of discriminatory policies against Japanese immigrants that spanned the first half of the twentieth century, and then by the dislocation of Japanese American communities on the West Coast during World War II. The wide range of discriminatory practices that separated Japanese Americans from real property complicates the prospects for preserving their landmarks.

While many places significant in Japanese American heritage have passed out of community control as a result of these historical processes, there is a case to be made for reasserting moral claims to places that are significant in Japanese American heritage. In light of the Diaspora, it is important to celebrate the rare examples where communities have retained access to their tangible heritage. There is also a pressing need to develop new strategies for interpreting the past and presenting it to the public at historic properties. If the real losses sustained by Americans of Japanese descent cannot fully be remedied, still the process of remembering includes reassembling many of the scattered, lost and broken pieces to gain a clearer understanding of what happened. Hopefully a deeper knowledge of this history will inspire new claims on the past, including a movement to preserve what remains of Japanese American heritage.

Chapter 1

SELLECK DISTRICT

Japanese Camp / **Selleck** / Washington

One of the best surviving examples of a western lumber mill town lies some twenty miles east and a little north of Tacoma, Washington, in the foothills of the Cascade Range. Sturdy bungalows that once housed Selleck's mill workers greet the rare visitor, as does the original community hall and an elementary school that now serves as an informal museum. Just out of town, all that remains of the historic sawmill is a towering incinerator, clearly visible in early panoramic photographs of the Pacific States Lumber Company, and part of the old engine room or powerhouse. Even in this fragmentary state, however, Selleck survives as a landmark of American labor history.

Unfortunately, the present boundaries of the Selleck Historic District exclude the site where Japanese mill workers encamped; yet it is an essential part of the area's history. Though most of the housing for Japanese workers was demolished after the mill went bankrupt during the Great Depression, recent research has identified some previously overlooked resources and much can be learned from the site's archaeological remains. These cultural resources, however, were not originally considered for inclusion in the historic district when it was listed on the National Register in 1989 because little was thought to remain, and the integrity of the Japanese camp paled in comparison with the sixteen homes of white workers that were standing. So too, the significance of Japanese immigrants in the lumber industry was poorly understood at the time the property was designated as a historic district.

Recent research focusing on the historical experiences of the Japanese at Selleck, drawn from archaeological remains and oral history interviews, among other sources, now provides a more accurate and complete picture of Japanese immigrants in the lumber industry. Taken together, this evidence suggests the need to widen the boundaries of the historic district to enhance the protection of Nikkei heritage and deepen

TOYO.
MAR. 1924

Far left, the remains of the incinerator. Above, Japanese workers and their families in Selleck, 1924.

Logging crew for the
No. 9 Snoqualmie Falls
Lumber Company.

the site's significance in terms of labor history by expanding our understanding of the diversity of the area's workforce.

From the enormous timbers used in shipbuilding to the standardized lumber dimensions that simplified residential construction in urban neighborhoods, a steady supply of wood from Pacific Northwest forests fueled western city building. While the majority of workers in Pacific Northwest mills were white men of Welsh, Irish, Italian, and Eastern European origins, it proved difficult to retain them in the remote mill towns that dotted the Cascades: Barneston, Eatonville, Onalaska, Ravensdale, Selleck, National, and Snoqualmie Falls, among others. Constant turnover led mill owners to begin recruiting Japanese immigrants toward the end of the nineteenth century. The Japanese reputedly were "reliable" workers, which in practice meant lower turnover, a willingness to work overtime, and distance from the kinds of unrest brought by labor unions. As a result, the earliest Japanese immigrants found steady work that paid better than most other types of employment open to the Issei (first generation of Japanese immigrants to America.)

More than one in five Japanese immigrants to America worked in the lumber industry in 1907. The U.S. Immigration Commission reported the presence of more than 2,000 Japanese in Washington State's lumber industry in 1909, employed in some sixty-seven mills and logging camps.[1] Railways operating in western forests employed many more Japanese as section hands and members of extra gangs. One laborer recalled carrying "my wicker trunk around with me from one sawmill to another railroad camp in Oregon, Wyoming, Utah and Idaho," where workers struggled with a poor diet, bedbugs, and outdoor work in scorching summer temperatures, while winters could reach twenty degrees below zero.[2]

Japanese bookmen facilitated the arrangements between American mill owners and Japanese workers, recruiting by word of mouth and notices posted in vernacular papers. Some bookmen raided railroad section crews for able-bodied workers. In the process, bookmen reputedly also kept an eye out for workers with superior hitting, catching, or pitching abilities to augment the lineup of the local baseball team. The bookman's duties included recruiting and supervising Japanese workers, keeping the books, and serving as an interpreter between labor and management.[3] He profited by collecting a fee from the workers and a commission from the merchants who served the camp. This arrangement disciplined Japanese labor as surely as the unions that organized white male workers.

Named after Frank L. Selleck, who supervised the land purchase and started the mill, the town of Selleck was built by the Pacific States Lumber Company between 1908 and 1916. A 1914 fire destroyed the original mill, but it was rebuilt, becoming one of the largest and best mills in Washington State. By 1919 the town had two hotels, a hospital, a school, a dance hall, saloons, and a number of stores. At its peak in the early 1920s, Selleck had grown to become one of the largest mill towns in the Northwest. In the late 1930s the Pacific States Lumber Company faced financial ruin due to a depressed lumber market and increased labor agitation. Forced into bankruptcy, the town was sold to creditors for $3,000 in 1940.

During more than thirty years of operation in Selleck, the Pacific States Lumber Company was typical in its reliance on a dual labor market that was stratified and segregated by race. The Japanese were hired into the lowest paid jobs and least skilled occupations, largely confined to outside work in an industry where the best paid jobs were located inside the mill, tending the machines. Japanese crews engaged in the heavy labor of sorting, grading, loading, and unloading lumber. Expert keel-piler Jun Ishii recalled the strain of lowering beams onto railroad cars, making piles eight feet wide and ten feet high. Three days into the job, he awoke unable to hold a rice bowl or bend his body.[4]

When Japanese immigrants were offered work in mill towns, they lived in racially segregated camps, often under inferior environmental conditions. In his 1924 report on "Orientals in the Lumber Industry," anthropologist Ronald Olson found that at twenty-two of the thirty-one mills he visited, Japanese camps were wholly separate from those that housed whites.[5] At the other nine mills, Japanese occupied a corner of the white settlement, suggesting that residential segregation by race was pervasive in the lumber industry. At the peak of production in the early 1920s, approximately 150 of the 600 to 700 men who were employed by the Pacific States Lumber Company were Japanese. Bachelors comprised approximately two-thirds of Japanese mill workers in Selleck, while the remaining one-third had families, with an average of 200 to 300 Japanese living in the camp during the 1920s and 1930s.

The Pacific States Lumber Company constructed housing for white workers around 1908. The fact that sixteen of the original twenty houses are still standing suggests that they were made of "solid timbers." In contrast, Japanese bachelors were crowded into rough bunkhouses. A description of one occupied by Japanese bachelors at Eatonville's sawmill, around 1918, suggests that as many as thirty to forty men bunked under one roof, two to a room.

Both Eatonville's and Selleck's Japanese camps had several bunkhouses. Their residents "took their meals at a central…cookhouse where hired cooks prepared meals for the boarders."[6] Standard fare was supplemented by comfort foods purchased from Seattle stores, "like bottles of pickled bean curd (funyu), salted sea urchin, fermented soy beans, salted plums, or seaweed preserved by boiling in soy sauce (nori no tsukudani)." The cookhouse at Selleck also contained a sento (public bathhouse.)

Pacific States Lumber Company in Selleck, Washington, 1916.

Asian crew at Camp No. 80,
Doty Lumber & Shingle Company,
Doty, Washington.

Above, the Japanese Language School at Selleck, 1924.

Selleck's Japanese families clustered near the tracks of the Chicago, Milwaukee, and St. Paul Railway line in crude dwellings built from scrap lumber provided by their employer.[7] Unlike bachelors, married men did not need to pay for personal services, since their wives cooked, did laundry, cut hair, and prepared hot baths in the family ofuro (soaking tub.) Although Japanese and white workers coexisted in racially divided communities, all of the children in Selleck attended a common elementary school.

The amenities were negligible in most company towns, particularly in the Japanese sections. Mill worker Isuke Miyazaki described his camp as "a remote spot many miles from human habitation, and it was terrifying how thousands of coyotes moved around in packs, howling."[8] Shoichiro Katsuno's camp reportedly was "vulgar and tasteless;" it possessed "no amusement whatsoever except the sound of the wind echoing among the hills and the whine of the milling machines."[9] Because going shopping in the nearest town or city took a day by train, workers eagerly awaited the arrival of provisions supplied by the Furuya Company and other Japanese importers. Older Nisei who worked as young men in the lumber mills remember salesmen from the import companies taking orders.[10] The goods were delivered by train or truck a week later and included fresh meat; fish, such as raw tuna for sashimi; canned seafood; rice; and ceramic cups and dishes.

Local white merchants resented the frugality of the Nikkei and wished they would spend more money at their stores. Japanese immigrants surely economized, maintaining their own gardens and chicken yards, and all but the worst gamblers saved money in order to send it home to Japan. But the repeated claim by white merchants that the Japanese and other Asian immigrants "lived on nothing" had little basis in fact. The Nikkei simply directed business to the Japanese companies that contracted their labor, which also supplied goods that were traditionally

The Japanese worker's camp, circa 1924.

Housing in the white section of Selleck has survived.

小間物及化粧具類

品名		直段
◯目醒時計	各種	一個 一、二五
◯懐中時計	同	一個 一〇、〇〇
◯時計鎖	同	一〇、〇
◯ケット	同	五、〇
◯ラクタイピン	同	二、〇
◯カウスボタン	同	五、〇
◯セフティーピン	同	五、〇
◯ブローチ	女用	三、五
◯カラーピン		一、七五
◯眼鏡	各用	五、〇
◯爪切鋏		一、二五
◯化粧具類	各種	一個
◯弗製手提袋	鹿皮製	一、五
◯絹製手提袋	横様入	一、二五
◯ハンドバッグ	カード入	二、五
◯ピン刺	新型様々	五、〇
◯糊斗	一打	二五
◯水引	大小色々	五〇

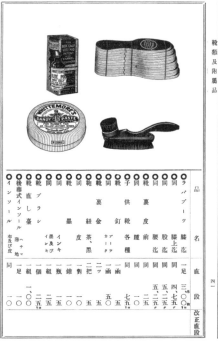

品名		直段 改正直段
◯ラバーブーツ	膝迄	三、〇
◯同 裏皮	腰迄	五、〇
◯同 裏皮	踵迄	四、五
◯鞄	各種	七、五
◯子供靴	各種	五、〇
◯靴釘 前金	一把	
◯同 裏金	一函	二、五
◯靴墨 茶、黒	一函	五、五
◯同 インキ及墨	一瓶	
◯靴直し臺	一個	一、五
◯検藤式インソール	一組	二、五
◯靴ブラシ 海ヘマ地	一足	
◯インソール 布及皮地		一、〇

四一

靴及附属品

品名		直段 改正直段
◯日用靴	同 一足	二、五
◯同 布製	同	二、七五
◯短靴 ゴム裏	同	一、五
◯運動靴 天	同	一、五
◯オーバシュー	同	一、六
◯日本スリッパ	同	一、五
◯スリッパ	同	一、五
◯労働靴 (極大)	同	三、五
◯麻裏草履 (大)	同	四、〇
◯絹 鼻緒	同	三、五
◯短靴 裏総金	同	二、五
◯同 赤皮	同	六、〇
◯長靴	一足	二、五

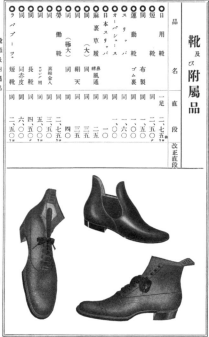

靴類及附属品

金物及砥石類

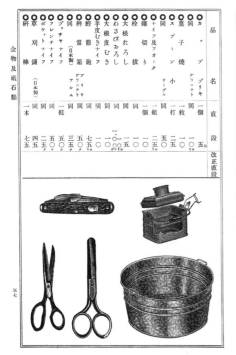

三七

品名		直段	改正直段
カップ　ブリキ		一個	七五
草刈鎌（日本製）		一本	四五
研棒			一五
ポケットナイフ		一挺	五〇
フレンチナイフ			三三
プチャナイフ		同	五〇
菓子焼		同	五〇
スプーン小　テーブル		一打	七五
鎌		一枚	一・五〇
切抜			二五
ナイフ及フォーク		一組	一・五〇
栓抜		一個	二五
大根おろし		同	五〇
大根皮むきナイフ		同	二五
わさびおろし		同	二五
芋皮むきナイフ		同	
鰹節鉋		同	五〇
辨當箱（日本製　アルミニット　ブリキ）		同	一五

品名		直段	改正直段
燒鍋		一個	三五
藥鍋（大小種々）		同	三〇
鍋 蓋		同	一五
鍋		同	一〇
茶焼（コーヒー）瓶		同	二五
フライパン 鐵製		一枚	一五
魚ロースバン		一個	一五
皿焼網		同	一〇
洗面器 ブリキ		同	三五
汁杓子 木柄付		同	一五
水杓子 ブリキ		同	一五
バケツ 小トタン		一本	八五
ワシュタップ 大小種々			二五

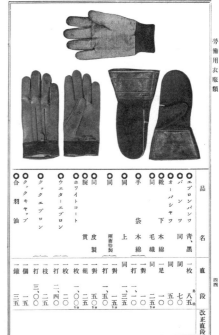

労働用衣服類

品名		直段	改正直段
エプロンパンツ 青、黒		一枚	八五
バンツ		同	一五
オーバシャツ		同	七五
靴下 木綿		一對	一五
靴下 毛織		一足	一〇
手袋 木綿		同	一五
手袋 上		同	二五
ウエターエプロン 皮製		一枚	一五
ホワイトコート 貫製		一枚	二・五〇
腕 縫附刺繡		一組	一五
クックエプロン		一枚	二五
クックキャップ		一打	三〇
合羽油		一個	三五
合羽		一鑵	三五

四四

Above, catalog of the M. Furuya Company, 1915.

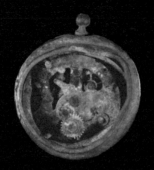

"I carried my wicker trunk with me, from one sawmill to another railroad camp in Oregon, Wyoming, Utah and Idaho."

ISUKE MIYAZAKI

JAPANESE RAILROAD AND LUMBER WORKER

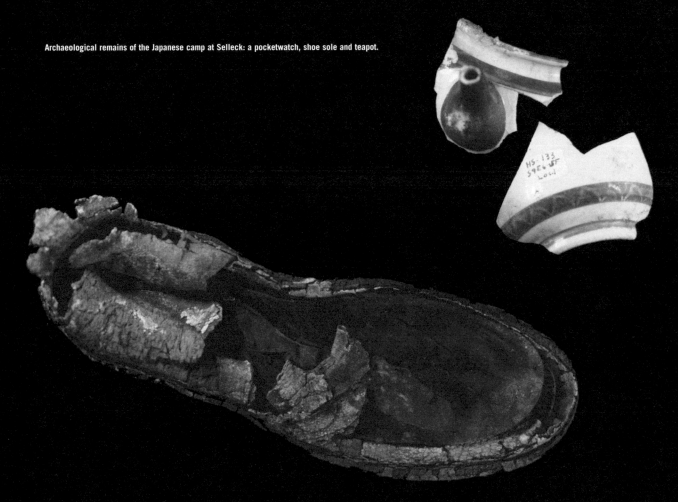

Archaeological remains of the Japanese camp at Selleck: a pocketwatch, shoe sole and teapot.

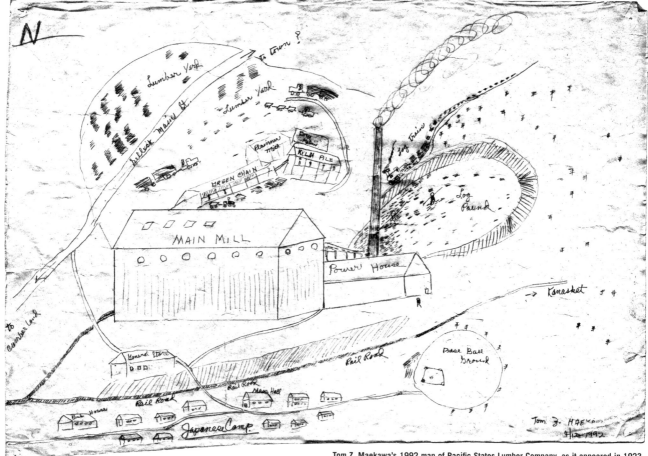

Tom Z. Maekawa's 1992 map of Pacific States Lumber Company, as it appeared in 1923.

a part of Japanese culture and diet, such as rice and shoyu (soy sauce), as well as basic supplies such as clocks, razors, pocketknives, boots, and work gloves.

In response to the spare conditions they encountered, Japanese immigrants developed some of their own social and cultural facilities in mill towns, such as the language school that Selleck's Nisei attended. Selleck's Japanese Hall accommodated gambling as well as the occasional motion picture. These activities surely made it more bearable to get through the long rainy and snowy winters, working out in the mill yard or log pond.

What is now known about the Japanese camp at Selleck is fragmentary at best. Surface artifacts, collected by Professor Gerald Hedlund and his students at Green River Community College in Auburn, Washington, offer clues about the goods Japanese workers used and consumed. A 1915 Furuya Company catalog is a valuable key to identifying these items: fragments of rice bowls, curled boot leather, a pocket watch, even a child's toy. Archaeologists Brad Bowden and Lynn Larson's preliminary analysis of Selleck's Japanese camp suggests that the site contains significant cultural resources that are worthy of protection, including two scatters of artifacts as well as a chimney and a cement pond associated with the home of Japanese foreman Frank Ozawa.[11]

Another key source for documenting the Japanese experience at Selleck is a map drawn by Tom Z. Maekawa. He returned, late in life, to show his family the place where he had worked as a young man. Drawn in 1992, the map represents his memory of Selleck in 1923. The map clearly depicts the process of converting logs to lumber, emphasizing the log pond and green chain where most of the Japanese worked, moving logs and lumber around the mill. This map is a remarkably accurate guide to locating the historic site of the Japanese camp, since it locates both the mill and the town's baseball diamond, which can be cross-referenced

with aerial photographs from the 1930s. Baseball, which figured prominently and pleasurably in the lives of Japanese mill workers, has proven critical for identifying the location of surviving cultural resources associated with Nikkei heritage.

Together, these sources increase our understanding of Japanese life and labor in the lumber industry. The evidence strongly suggests that Japanese immigrants are important, not peripheral, figures in the history of Selleck and other Pacific Northwest mill towns. Archaeologists Bowden and Larson, therefore, have argued that the boundaries of the Selleck Historic District should be expanded to include the site of the Japanese camp, which would protect all of the archaeological remains and aboveground artifacts.

A recent study identified Selleck as a possible National Historic Landmark based on its importance in American labor history. Widening the boundaries of the Selleck Historic District to include the Japanese camp would provide a more accurate and complete picture of the past, while recognition as a landmark would bring increased public awareness of its significance. Selleck is a great untapped resource for educating the public about the dynamics of race, class, ethnicity, and gender within American labor history — complex themes often addressed in contemporary scholarship but rarely voiced in the public venue of historic sites and buildings.

Considering the rough conditions that lumber workers and members of railroad section crews encountered in rather isolated sawmill towns and camps, it is little wonder that so many Issei left the woods, sent to Japan for wives, and took up farming in rural areas. There they grew a variety of vegetables and berries, and operated dairy farms. The farms also proved to be a fertile environment for raising their children, the Nisei or second generation. Although individual trajectories varied, many of the Nisei traversed the twentieth century spending their childhood on farms, their youth in internment camps, and the remainder of their adult lives — in the postwar period — in American cities and suburbs. Yet there are few historic places in the American West where it is possible to learn about the rural dimensions of Japanese American life in the years before internment.

The Neely Mansion, located on Auburn-Black Diamond Road in the historic White River Valley of Western Washington, is a house museum with great potential to raise public awareness and appreciation of the Nikkei's part in American agricultural history in the first half of the twentieth century. To achieve that potential, the past interpretive focus on the initial period of construction, ownership, and occupancy of the mansion by the Neely family necessarily has expanded to include the property's longer history and embrace its multicultural heritage. But there is still much to be done.

The Neely Mansion was built by Aaron Neely and his father, David, in 1894. David and Irene Kemp Neely had migrated from Tennessee with their three young sons in 1854, becoming some of the first white pioneers in the White River Valley.[1] The family homesteaded northwest of the present city of Kent, carving a farm out of the landscape. Aaron remained on the family farm until he married Sarah Graham in 1876, piecing together 120 acres of land just east of the town of Auburn. They removed the Douglas firs from the property and sold the heavy timber, transforming the land into a well-organized farm with an orchard and a herd of sixty Holstein cows. When their original log cabin became too small for the Neelys and their large family, they built a new residence on the property.

Drawing on their Tennessee roots, Aaron and his father designed and built the new dwelling in the style of a southern mansion. The Aaron Neely family moved into the house in 1894, living there for more than a decade. They ultimately left the farm in 1908 for a new house in Auburn, where they enjoyed modern amenities including electricity and indoor plumbing. From 1908 on, the Neelys rented out the farm to a succession of Swiss, Japanese, and finally Filipino tenants, until the house was designated a landmark, restored to its original condition, and opened as a historic house museum. Listed on the National Register of Historic Places in 1974, the Neely Mansion was only the second property to become a King County Landmark when it was designated in 1983. The mansion gained recognition based on its association with the pioneering family as well as its architecture,

which was judged at the time to be "the most elaborate piece of craftsman architecture in unincorporated King County."[2]

From that point on, the Neely Mansion Association focused primarily (though by no means exclusively) on the legacy of the Neely family, restoring the house to its original appearance. To the association's credit, volunteer docents have for years told visitors what they know about the tenants who lived in the house and farmed the property after the Neelys left. A 1926 photograph, for example, that hangs in the parlor of the Neely Mansion prompts docents to talk about the Fukuda family, who ran a dairy ranch on the Neely property from 1912 to 1930. The recent recovery of an outbuilding — which housed an ofuro (Japanese bath) — will serve as a touchstone for telling visitors about the Horis, who were the second Japanese family to farm the property. More could be done, of course, to "make the invisible visible," as planning historian Leonie Sandercock has termed the process of recovering the lost history of marginalized groups. Fortunately, the Neely Mansion Association is committed to preserving the bathhouse and augmenting the interpretive program at the historic house museum.[3]

The stories of subsequent tenants have been pieced together in the past decade by graduate students in historic preservation at the University of Washington, who discovered the Hori furoba as part of a 1994 class project,[4] and by historian Mildred Andrews, who prepared a county landmark nomination for the bathhouse in 1996.[5] New research to collect relevant documents, records, oral history interviews, and photographs held in private collections has begun to fill gaps in the history of the Neely property.

When Aaron and his wife, Sarah, moved off the property, the Galli family prepared to move into the Neely Mansion. Their story is relatively well documented.[6] Ernst and Hannah Simu Galli were Swiss and Swedish immigrants, respectively, who came across the Atlantic as teenagers, eventually leasing the Neely property in 1908. Life on the farm was tough, as indicated by the fact that Hannah worked right up to childbirth, cooking the usual noon meal for all the farmhands on the day that her son was born. It took so long for her husband to come in from the haying, after Hannah's labor started, that Arnold Galli Sr. had already made his debut. Five years after they began leasing the Neely property, the Gallis bought their own farm north of Auburn. This option would not be readily available to the succession of Japanese tenants who leased the Neely property from 1912 until World War II because of racially restrictive land laws and discriminatory practices.

A mill worker in Yakima who emigrated from Japan to the United States in 1902, Matasuke Fukuda was one of the many Japanese who left the lumber industry to marry and establish farms in the White River Valley. There he joined other immigrants from Hiroshima Prefecture. Matasuke and his wife, Toku, took the Gallis' place at the Neely Mansion in 1912, ultimately living there for nearly two decades and raising ten children. Their son Sentaro (Sam) bolstered the family's skills and confidence in this new line of work by undertaking a two-year apprenticeship

with a white dairy farmer. Despite the size of the Fukuda family, the large scope of their operation — with some 200 to 300 cows, plus corn and rhubarb — required substantial help from white and Filipino laborers.

Japanese settlement of the White and Puyallup River Valleys had begun approximately two decades before the Fukudas decided to move there from Yakima. According to one of historian Kazuo Ito's sources, the first Japanese to enter dairy farming in the White River Valley was Gentaro Ikeda of Hiroshima Prefecture, who established an operation in Kent. Ikeda later formed a finance association and organized the Seattle Milk (Shippers') Association to promote the economic interests of his kinsmen. By 1907, 147 families had settled in the valley.

The number of Japanese-operated dairies in the area skyrocketed between 1910 and 1920, increasing from thirteen to eighty dairies total.[7] The local condensed milk plants established by the Borden and Carnation companies gave dairy farmers in the White River Valley the confidence needed to expand their herds. The establishment in 1916 of the Japanese-operated White River Creamery in Kent, which processed milk, cheese, and butter for shipment to Seattle and Spokane, mitigated anti-Japanese agitation in Borden and Carnation's condensing plants, while directly connecting Japanese farmers with a wider market. This led to an unprecedented period of prosperity for the area's Japanese dairy farmers, who reportedly supplied about half of the fresh dairy products that Seattle residents consumed. Home to a large segment of the state's Japanese population, the White River Valley had become

A Japanese Farm in the
Black River Valley, Washington

Photo by Nowell & Rognan, Seattle.

Japanese farms were barely distinguishable from those run by their white neighbors on account of the need to hide Japanese property interests.

the rural center of Nikkei settlement in Washington by 1920, with a cluster of community institutions such as churches and language schools.[8]

Yet success in agriculture did not lead to widespread land ownership for Japanese immigrants, as one might reasonably expect; in fact, the opposite was true. The 90 percent rate of leasing by Japanese in the White River Valley recorded in 1941 reflects the pervasive influence of discriminatory property laws on social relations of race, class and ethnicity. The Washington State Constitution and the passage of the Alien Land Laws in the early 1920s limited Japanese immigrants to leasing land; they could, however, evade the law by placing ownership in the hands of their Nisei children, a white ally, or a dummy corporation.

The rise in anti-Japanese sentiment in the years that followed World War I led many Japanese to leave agriculture, prompted by the enforcement of the Alien Land Laws and the terror of racially motivated arsons that destroyed the barns and fertilizer plants of many White River Valley Japanese farmers. A slump in milk prices during the years immediately following the war and an increase in the (discriminatory) inspection of Japanese dairy herds forced many Nikkei farmers to sell their livestock at a substantial loss and leave the business. Some former dairy farmers diversified, cultivating berries, peas, cauliflower, and other goods that could be shipped east by rail or sold at Seattle's Pike Place Market. Others moved on, resettling in urban areas, where they joined their kinsmen in Nihonmachi (Japantowns.) The decline in milk prices contributed to the Fukudas' decision to leave the Neely property in 1930. Some family members returned to Japan for several years, while others settled permanently in California.

In 1930 Shigeichi Hori moved onto the Neely property, where he farmed with his wife, Shimanoko, and their children (four sons and one daughter) for the better part of a decade. It was not the first place that they had farmed in the area. The son of a farmer in Hiroshima Prefecture, Shigeichi Hori had left Japan for the United States in 1907 at the age of fifteen. His first employment was as a milker for a white farmer in Orillia, Washington.[9] The fact that it took him "more than one year to become competent at milking twenty-five to thirty cows a day" suggests that the skills required for dairy farming did not always come easily.[10] A formal family portrait taken for a book celebrating the accomplishments of Nikkei from Hiroshima Prefecture shows the Horis at the place they farmed in Kent before moving to the Neely property. The picture was composed so that the signs of their economic achievements dominated: farm, barn, automobile, and dairy herd. The proud parents appear in an inset (see overleaf).

When Shigeichi Hori's brother and sister-in-law left Japan in 1920 to help with the farm, the White River Valley was the most active center of farming for the Japanese in Washington State, with over 4,000 cows grazing on nearly 3,000 acres. Yet in spite of the economic opportunity posed by working on the Kent dairy farm, Jitsuo Otoshi judged the work harshly, describing it as "hard and long." If uprooting massive stumps with dynamite qualified as hard work in the context of Nikkei farmsteads, employment as a milker on the Horis' dairy farm also posed hardships, in Otoshi's assessment, particularly since there were no holidays and sick leave was nonexistent, unless the milker turned violently ill. Like Hori, Otoshi found it hard to master the art of milking.

As soon as I arrived at [Hori's farm] I became a milker for him. Just watching someone squeeze out milk looks easy enough, but when you try it yourself it is quite tricky…Even after I had mastered the secret of it and could milk skillfully enough, my hands ached even the next morning; they swelled up like a pancake and I couldn't bend my fingers.[11]

NIKKEI FROM HIROSHIMA

The photograph at left shows Shigeichi and Shimanoko Hori, as featured in a 1919 photographic survey of western Washington celebrating the accomplishments of Nikkei from Hiroshima Prefecture in Japan. Note the rare example of an irimoya (gable into hipped) roof, a traditional Asian architectural form, topping the Horis' dairy barn.

A combination of pride and fear underlay the decision of Seattle's Hiroshima kenjinkai (prefectural association) to produce this extensive photographic survey of the accomplishments of its membership. Clearly, Japanese residents of the cities of Seattle and Tacoma, as well as the hinterlands of Kent, Sumner, Puyallup, and Auburn, were apprehensive that California's Alien Land Law of 1913 might spread north to Washington. They hoped photographic documentation of their homes and businesses would persuade the Japanese government to redouble its efforts to protect them from the passage of similar legislation. Nevertheless, Washington's Alien Land Laws of 1921 and 1923 were enacted shortly after the book was published.

Yet there was no time off to recover, "so trying to ignore the pain I went on squeezing." It took six months before Jitsuo was conditioned to the work.

Routinely operating with only five hours of sleep, the dairy workers were dependent on alarm clocks to wake them at 3 am for the day's first milking. The milkers sat down to breakfast afterward. The second milking took place around 3 pm, preferably after the dairy workers had slept a bit. Little wonder that they tended to complain about interrupted sleep, as well as sore hands.[12]

The Horis leased the Neely property from 1930 to 1940, during which time they kept only a small herd, since they already had experienced failure in the dairy business during the 1920s. In place of a larger herd, they concentrated on growing fruits and vegetables, including strawberries and rhubarb. Shigeichi Hori worked as a buyer for the F. H. Hogue Packing Company in Kent, where he had farmed previously. His brother and sister-in-law tended the farm, living in a second house on the Neely property. In an interview with historian Mildred Andrews, the Horis' daughter Mary (Hori) Nakamura remembered that they also sold strawberries from a roadside stand. Three times a week, after public school, Mary and her brothers attended language school at the Auburn Buddhist Temple.

Shigeichi Hori clearly suffered from the combination of forces that undercut nearly all Japanese farmers in the interwar period: the slump in milk prices, the increase in hostile inspections, and the passage of the Alien Land Laws. As a result of these pressures, he "auctioned off the cows along with the equipment and tools," incurring debts that took him more than a decade to clear.[13] Shigeichi Hori and his immediate family moved off the Neely property in 1936, opening a grocery in Kent. His brother and sister-in-law stayed on the Neely property until World War II internment.

Left, Berry pickers in Kent, Washington. Above, Seattle's Pike Place Market. Japanese predominated at the Pike Place Market prior to World War II.

Aaron Neely's family moved in briefly thereafter, out of desperation, since they had a difficult time finding new tenants with all of the Japanese gone. Within several years, they left and the Neely property entered a new phase of its history under Filipino tenants, a period that would last until its eventual designation as a landmark.

In 1994, Pedro (also known as Pete) and June Acosta recalled their part in the history of the Neely Mansion for Stacy Patterson, a University of Washington graduate student in planning and preservation.[14] After working for some years as a migrant laborer in the heat of California's agricultural districts (in places such as Oxnard, Ventura, and Salinas), Pete Acosta came to the White River Valley on the eve of America's entry into World War II. He first farmed upriver from the Neelys, but in 1943 took a lease on the property. He was joined several years later by his new bride, June. As June tells the story, she first met Pete at the East Highway Garage, where she worked. He needed a tractor fixed. Their interracial relationship, Filipino-Caucasian, was common enough that the couple remembered few problems. After they married, Pete and June lived in a house on the Neely property with their daughter, Juliana, who was born in 1946. The Acostas grew a wide array of produce, with strawberries as a mainstay.

June, Juliana and Pete Acosta, 1948

While the Acostas lived in a second house on the property, changes in the uses of the mansion and the outbuildings marked a transition from Japanese to Filipino tenancy in this period. The mansion was subdivided into separate bedrooms, essentially functioning as a rooming house for Filipino laborers. This living arrangement reflected the male nature of Filipino migrant worker society, which in turn stemmed from immigration restrictions on Filipino women. Through the liberal use of chicken wire, the tenants converted the attic into a coop for pigeons or squab, which they cooked. The men kept fighting cocks in the former rhubarb shed.

Most of the men who occupied the Neely Mansion during the Acostas' tenure were migrant laborers who circulated among and between White River Valley farmsteads; the bunkhouses of Alaska canneries; and the single room occupancy hotels of Seattle, such as the NP and the Panama. For that reason, Pete and June remember only their first names: Surio; Mariano; Pat; Alec; (Young) Tony; (Old) Tony; and Ace, who was the last to move off the property in the 1970s.[15]

It was in this period of Filipino occupancy that the furoba built by Shigeichi Hori became obsolete for cultural reasons. Immediately adjacent to the Neely Mansion stood a 10' x 16' wood frame shed, which had served as the Hori family's traditional Japanese bathhouse. According to Mary (Hori) Nakamura, whose father had built the furoba when they moved into the Neely Mansion in 1930,

The Japanese bath had a wooden tub with a metal bottom and a board in the tub so that we could soak in the tub without getting burned. A fire was built under the tub to heat the water in the tub.

While the Western practice was to wash in the bath water, the traditional Japanese practice involved scrubbing and rinsing outside of the tub before soaking in the scalding hot water.

Neither Pete Acosta nor the other Filipinos who occupied the Neely property after 1943 had much use for the bathhouse — particularly in the form that it had been used by past tenants — since their bathing practice was to stand and pour heated water over their heads. So too, the Acostas' house, built in 1942 and remodeled during the 1960s, had its own bathing facilities. Consequently, after bracing the structure, Pete hitched the shed to his tractor and dragged it some seventy-five feet west of the mansion, where it stood until University of Washington planning and preservation students discovered it in the course of documenting the past presence of Asian Americans at the Neely property.

Long abandoned (when it was rediscovered, it was actually sitting on a separate parcel from that occupied by the Neely Mansion), the furoba nevertheless was in sufficiently good condition to merit designation as a King County Landmark when it was nominated in 1996. Designation paved the way for the bathhouse to be returned to its proper place beside the mansion, as it appeared in a 1939 photograph. While the shed's frame, in carpenters' terms, no longer was "square and true" and important interior features such as the ofuro (soaking tub) had long been missing, the shed clearly was the bathhouse that Shigeichi Hori had built for his family in 1930.

The surviving bathhouse is an evocative reminder of the past presence of Japanese tenants on the farmstead, as well as a touchstone for future interpretation. Mildred Andrews, who prepared the landmark nomination for the Hori furoba, also noted the presence of surviving fruit trees from the Neelys' old apple and cherry orchards. Even when considered together, the house,

Juliana Acosta, 1948

furoba, and surrounding landscape still may not be enough to invoke the whole spirit of the historic farmstead, where hundreds of dairy cows grazed during the Fukudas' tenancy and acres of berries, orchards, hothouse rhubarb, and other produce filled the fields during the Horis' time, as well as later during the Acostas' residence. According to Mildred Andrews, many of the outbuildings, such as "the large cow barn, a milk house, a horse stable, a smokehouse, a silo, a garage, and a workers' house," are long gone. Others, such as the Acostas' residence, which was damaged in a fire department training exercise, survive in a derelict state. A drastic reduction in the overall size of the Neely property, now just half an acre, gives the house a prominence in the immediate landscape that is somewhat misleading in historical terms. Fortunately, surrounding farmland — saved by King County's agricultural and forest protection program — provides a visual context for the historic house as well as a buffer to protect it from the wave of post-agricultural development that is sweeping the valley. The recovery of the Hori furoba further enhances the interpretive context for the Neely Mansion.

The Neely Mansion is only one of many historic properties where a new awareness of the nation's multicultural past suggests the need for reinterpretation. New approaches to interpretation will recognize the imprints of multiple ethnic groups on the landscape: in forests, on farms, in camps, in towns, in cities and in suburbs. Well-established preservation practices also merit rethinking when they get in the way of telling "the whole story," to use public historian Heather Huyck's phrase. The decision to restore the physical fabric of the Neely Mansion to its earliest period of use might warrant reexamination in light of a multitiered approach to interpretation that reaches across more than a century to embrace the stories of the Swiss, Japanese, and Filipino tenants who lived and worked there. Certainly there are some historic places for

Above, Neely Mansion with adjacent furoba, 1939.
Right, Hori Furoba, as rediscovered in 1994.

Neely Mansion, as seen from
Auburn-Black Diamond Road, 1994.

which the period of significance should remain much more limited. Battlefields and other sites of tragedy, for example, often gain their significance in a week, day, or moment. But the real interpretive power of the Neely property lies in its layers of use, over a long time period, by diverse groups.

The White River Valley, along with Bellevue, Bainbridge Island, Vashon Island, and numerous other locales, enjoy a wealth of Japanese American resources that merit inventory and protection by preservation agencies. These resources are so numerous, and so widely scattered throughout the western region, that they merit consideration as a wider heritage area or multiple property nomination for the purposes of preservation planning and protection.

Aaron Neely's claim to a place in history as a member of one of the valley's pioneer white families seems like a dubious achievement when viewed through the sharper lens of multicultural awareness. The more inclusive version of the Neely Mansion's history, however, suggests that historic houses have untapped potential to challenge biased and outmoded notions about whose history matters. The hope is that fourth grade students in Mrs. Carpenter's class at nearby Neely-O'Brien Elementary School, who in past years constructed a web page devoted to the Neely family's history at the mansion, will soon recognize that the mansion's tenants paralleled the diversity that they experience on an everyday basis. Perhaps the broader lesson to be learned from this act of reinterpretation is that rather than freezing historic houses at idealized moments in time, we might adopt a richer approach that emphasizes changing social relations over longer periods of time. It also suggests that tenants, laborers, servants, and slaves, as well as property owners, deserve to be included in the formal portraits that typically hang in the parlors of historic house museums.

Chapter 3

NATSUHARA'S STORE

622 West Main Street / **Auburn** / Washington

七福神

Interior of Natsuhara's store, 1997.

"Frank Natsuhara's grocery store on Main Street in Auburn is much the same as it was when his father, Chiyokichi, opened it about sixty-five years ago," began a 1980 story in the Kent, Washington, *Daily News Journal.* "There's an old rolltop desk in the corner piled with order blanks and paperwork, antique glass and mahogany display cabinets, a big steel safe and a handsome bronze cash register."[1] Or, as one of his relatives used to say, with a little hint of exasperation, "Uncle Frank never threw anything away!" For that reason, he also was an important resource for those studying the history of the region.

Over the years, the dry goods, hay, grain, and feed store had given way to a gift shop. The counter of Natsuhara's store was cluttered with an eclectic display of Japanese fans and American flags. Valuable old photographs and inexpensive gifts crowded the shelves. More than a decade and a half after the 1980 newspaper article was written, its description remained current, though the man and the store both showed a few signs of age. With his bedroom upstairs and his kitchen in back, Frank led the modest life of a devout Buddhist, longtime widower, devoted family member, and unofficial historian in a place that once had been less than welcoming to its Japanese American residents. "Live long enough…" he would say, not finishing the thought. But what he hinted at was the irony of it all: no matter how poorly some local people had treated him when they were younger, most locals relied upon him in old age as a repository of community memory.

His death on April 6, 1999, at the age of 88 was a sad occasion for the many who knew him. This loss was compounded four months later when the store and virtually all of its contents burned to the ground in an arson-related fire.[2] While it is no longer possible to mark the contributions of the Natsuhara family at their store, which stood for more than eighty years (from 1916 to 1999) at 622 West Main Street in Auburn, Washington, their story is an important chapter in Nikkei heritage, and their store represents a vanishing property type that deserves to be documented.

In 1876, Frank's father, Chiyokichi Natsuhara, was born in Shiga Prefecture, Japan. Less than a decade later, his mother, Sen Furukawa, was born in a nearby village. Leaving home in his early twenties, Chiyokichi entered the United States illegally through Canada. During those first few years, he laid track for the railroad. Frank recalled hearing stories about the rough conditions under which the railroad gangs of his father's generation labored, barely subsisting on "salt water soup and

Frank Natsuhara, 1997.

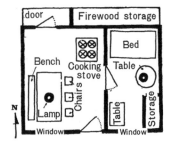

**Chiyokichi and Sen Natsuhara's
first home in rural Auburn, 1905**

flour-paste dumplings" before import companies such as Furuya began to supply them with more appealing provisions. Around 1902 Chiyokichi left railroad work and took up farming in the vicinity of Christopher, where other kinsmen had settled. There he farmed potatoes, cabbage, and berries. After more than six years — from age twenty-three to thirty — living in the Northwest as a bachelor, Chiyokichi wrote to his family in Japan, asking their help in finding him a bride who was "healthy and tall in stature, and able to read and write letters."[3]

Twenty-year-old Sen Furukawa, who lived in the next village to Chiyokichi's family, answered his request. As she later recalled the beginnings of their relationship:

My [future] husband, Chiyokichi, was a cousin of my step-aunt, but even though he was related to me, I had not previously known him. I felt slightly uneasy to marry a person I never knew except through a picture, but my grandparents had seen him once, and as they said he would be all right, I believed in them and so decided to marry him.[4]

For each to have moved to America and marry was rather unusual, since both were first-born children with significant responsibilities for the care of their parents.[5] Leaving Japan and following a long difficult crossing of the Pacific Ocean by ship, she eventually arrived in Seattle. After an on-board wedding ceremony to satisfy U.S. immigration officials, the newlyweds headed for their new home. "In Auburn," Sen recalled, "a new house was waiting for us. It was a humble house, which my husband built with the help of three or four friends, using about $50 worth of materials. It had only two rooms, bedroom and a kitchen."[6]

If married life in rural Auburn represented an improvement for Chiyokichi, Sen perceived it as a giant step backwards. Her new living conditions were more miserable than the worst rural poverty in her home prefecture:

I had to carry the water every day, in buckets or oil cans, as the well was about 200 feet from the house, on the landlord's property. We heated the water outside of the house for washing and bathing. The toilet was about 100 feet behind the house. As to our new abode, there were many open spaces between the boards in the wall. One night I burned the stove and burned

*the stove, and yet the house didn't warm up, so I got plenty of old newspapers from the land-
lord, and making a flour paste I papered double over the worst places. When I was burning
some home-made charcoal in the room to dry the newspaper, I got a headache so I immediately
opened the door and, feeling the cold wind, I went outside and ate snow. After that I felt easy
again. Apparently I had been about to die from the carbon monoxide in the room. In this way
my life in America began.*[7]

Many early Japanese immigrants to the White River Valley and nearby Bainbridge and Vashon
Islands did the backbreaking work of clearing stump land for crops; others ran dairy farms.

The 1911 birth of their eldest son, Senji, also known as Frank, coincided with the Natsuharas'
establishment of a store in their Christopher farmhouse. One room, declared off-limits to the
children, was used to store rice, tea, and soy sauce purchased in Seattle for resale in Auburn.
By 1914 Chiyokichi Natsuhara had arranged to import rice and tea directly from Japan, selling goods
on credit during the winter to Japanese farmers, who settled their debt after the harvest.

By 1917, the Natsuharas had built and opened a store in Auburn on West Main Street near
the Union Pacific tracks and the family had moved in upstairs. With their truck, the Natsuharas'
supplied Japanese families farming in the surrounding areas of Auburn, Kent, Puyallup, Parkland,
Sumner, as well as in Bellevue, Orting, and Vashon and Bainbridge Islands. Farm supplies also went
to Renton, farms around Seattle such as those in the Greenlake area, and beyond.[8] The Natsuharas
sold hay, grain, feed and fertilizer out of their warehouse. Sen ran the store, which sold dry goods,
Japanese specialty foods and medicines, buttonhole shoes, yardage and various provisions.

To distinguish the store from its competitors, Chiyokichi and Sen imported the highest
quality tea from their home prefecture and brought over a rice polishing machine.[9] The rice was
shipped from Japan to Auburn unhulled because there was a significant import tax on Japanese
white rice, so it was more profitable to finish the polishing process at the point of purchase.
Frank recalled that operating the rice polishing machine was his "mother's work. I had to run out
here (from the warehouse to the store) every once in a while and grab a sample, bring it to her
and she'd say: 'Oh, we've got to run it through some more.'" Repeating the polishing process
ensured a first-class product.

Chiyokichi and Sen Natsuhara, 1909

SEN NATSUHARA

Hinamatsuri or Girls' Day, which occurs annually on the third of March, was the focus of Sen Natsuhara's considerable talents as a doll-maker. On that occasion, Japanese girls formally displayed their dolls on stepped shelves, including Emperor, Empress, and their court. Despite long workdays on the farm and at the store, Sen provided most of her daughters with an original set of dolls, as this excerpt from a March 2, 1951 letter Sen sent to her daughter Tomiko indicates.

Dear Tomiko,
How is everyone? We are OK here. Last year I made the Emperor and Empress dolls for Reiko (granddaughter Sandra's Japanese name). This year I made the three Ladies in Waiting. I have been busy putting up blackberry cane vine. I'm tired but little by little worked on making these dolls in the nighttime until 2 am when it was snowing and this morning there was frost. I'm just finished making these dolls so sending this package at the post office on March 2nd, but it will not get there in time for March 3rd.

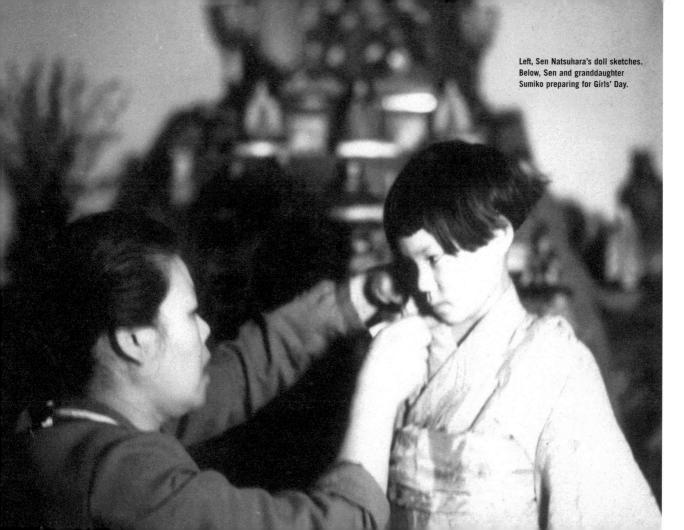

Left, Sen Natsuhara's doll sketches.
Below, Sen and granddaughter
Sumiko preparing for Girls' Day.

Chiyokichi and Sen had a large family of eleven children, not all of whom survived to adulthood, although they themselves lived into their nineties. One of the first lessons their children learned was that the more they helped, the sooner they would be able to go out and play. On weekdays the family carved out an existence living and working at the Auburn store; the children attended public school in town. On weekends they lived at the Christopher farm, where they worked several fields, around forty acres of blackberries, and where their fertilizer mixing plant was located.

Chiyokichi and Sen took turns traveling back and forth to Japan to supply the store and visit their families. Sen returned from one trip with 250 two-to-three inch koi. The family built an extraordinary Japanese garden and pond at their Christopher residence, having visited showplaces such as the Mukais' garden on Vashon Island for ideas and gathering enormous rocks from all around. The Natsuhara children remember both the strain of moving the rocks as well as their evocative quality. The grandchildren remember feeding leftover rice to the fish after dinner.

Typically, the Natsuharas took one or more children with them to Japan. Upon their arrival, those who made the journey (Chise, Frank, Sekiko, Tomiko and Jack) were surprised to discover that they would be staying for one to three years with their relatives while their parent returned home to America. But it was an opportunity for them to get to know their grandparents and other relatives while absorbing Japanese language and traditional cultural practices such as flower arrangement, tea ceremony and koto playing.

The Natsuharas sold crates, bought berries, and shipped them to eastern Washington, Wyoming, and Montana by rail. The whole family participated in the construction of the berry boxes, with the help of laborers who lived in a series of rooms alongside the store. As Frank later recalled:

At one time, [in the 1920s], during the winter and spring, couples who worked for my dad stayed in the apartments beside the store. All they had was electricity. The water was outside and a Japanese-style bath was in the back. They made berry crates all winter that we piled up in the warehouse; in the spring we'd haul them out to the farms. During the summer, the people who had assembled berry crates for us would work on the farms and in the fall, they'd come back.

Frank's sister Maryo also remembered the elaborate berry crate construction process:

The men would be making the crates, nailing them together, while the women were stapling the wooden berry cups by the thousands, throwing them into big piles. We all had individual machines. When the children came home from public school and Japanese language class, they would see all the work being done. Their job was to assemble twelve or twenty-four cups to a crate, stack them up to be moved to a different part of the warehouse, ready for sale or delivery to all the farms. There was always lots of work to be done, including preparing supplies for the next day's work.

Immigration hearings held in Seattle and Tacoma document rising anti-Japanese sentiment around 1920.[10] Some white neighbors were extremely uncomfortable with the growing concentration of Japanese immigrants in the White River Valley, particularly in the dairy industry, and by 1922 anti-Asian groups were organizing locally.[11] Harassing inspections of dairy herds on Japanese farms, as well as a wave of suspicious arson fires, suggest the backlash was aimed at undermining the achievements of Japanese farmers.

Natsuhara family portrait, circa 1935. Left to right: George, Maryo, Frank, Tomiko, Chiyokichi (patriarch), Jack, Sen (matriarch),

Couples who worked for my dad stayed in the apartments beside the store. All they had was electricity. The water was outside and a Japanese-style bath was in the back. They made berry crates all winter that we'd pile up in the warehouse; in the spring we'd haul them out to the farms. During the summer, the people who had assembled berry crates for us would work on the farms and in the fall, they'd come back."

FRANK NATSUHARA

OWNER, NATSUHARA'S ORIENTAL IMPORTS

Late in life, Sen described the series of arsons that terrorized Japanese farmers in the Kent-Auburn area in the 1920s and 1930s. The fires first claimed the Kosai dairy barns; then the farm of Buichiro Itabashi, burning their cows alive; then the Yasumura dairy barns; and finally, the Natsuharas' fertilizer mixing and storage building.[12] One Saturday night around 10:30pm, Sen and her children noticed a glow in the darkness by their large warehouse across the field. They saw a suspicious car drive away as the warehouse burst into flames. The arson fire destroyed the building down to its concrete foundation.

Political efforts to ward off Washington State's Alien Land Laws proved unsuccessful, and, their passage in 1921 and 1923 made it illegal to sell or lease land to a non-U.S. citizen, meaning they were designed to inhibit Issei agricultural holdings. Nevertheless, many Issei persevered, leasing land in the name of their American-born children or making arrangements with sympathetic white neighbors.

The Natsuhara family's experience embodies many broad patterns in Japanese American history, including the effects of local implementation of Alien Land Laws. Kazuo Ito documented the little-known fact that the Natsuharas, along with their neighbors, the Maekawas, were prosecuted for an alleged violation. Chiyokichi Natsuhara and Otokichi Maekawa jointly leased eight acres from an American citizen in 1916 under a ten year contract. The passage and increasing enforcement of the Alien Land Law in the early 1920s threw into question the validity of their long term lease. At trial, fortunately, Natsuhara and Maekawa won. But, interestingly enough, decades later, when Sen was interviewed by Ito for a history of the Japanese American community, she had no knowledge of the case. Even though at the time of the trial she had been married and living with her husband for more than ten years, Sen noted with a mixture of denial and dismay,

My husband never told me that he was accused for violation of the Alien Land Law.... I who shared 60 years with him, including joys and sorrows, could never have missed such a thing.[13]

As Ito reluctantly notes, however, the trial is a matter of historical record. One of Frank's sisters attributed the silence to the men's attempts to shelter women from any kind of trouble. If the women did not know about the intricacies of the property deals, they might not be prosecuted. The Natsuharas' property nominally was owned by their American-born children: the Auburn store by their eldest son, Frank, and the Christopher property by the youngest boys, Jack and George.

If these direct attacks on the community weren't enough, other consequences of racial discrimination took their toll. Living and working "on the other side of the tracks" involved real environmental hazards for Japanese settlers, who repeatedly risked life and limb at railroad and street car crossings.[14] On August 18, 1911, while Sen Natsuhara was napping, her three year old daughter, Yuko, and a sister left without permission to show Yuko's new shoes to their father, Chiyokichi. Crossing nearby railroad tracks, one of Yuko's shoes got caught. She was killed by an interurban train as she tried to recover her shoe. Sen never took a nap again. Frank later lost his wife Shizuko to a similar fate in a collision between her car and a train. All of this makes a surviving picture of the Natsuhara children sledding near the tracks a rather haunting image.

By the time of Frank's thirteenth birthday, in 1924, it was his responsibility to drive the company truck out of town to surrounding Japanese farms to gather orders from the women. "They'd buy rice and whatever you had to present," he freely recalled. "In those days women never left their home. The men were the only ones that moved around." Bound to farm and ranch by their children, immigrant women in outlying areas

Natsuhara children sledding in the mid-1930s.

Young Frank Natsuhara out making deliveries in the 1920s.

enjoyed limited help, even from midwives. The delivery trucks sent out by import companies provided Northwest Nikkei with a slender connection to the goods and services of larger Japanese American communities. This was particularly true for Japanese located in small town, rural, and wilderness areas, allowing them to maintain a somewhat traditional diet (that included fish, tofu, shoyu, and miso).

As the Great Depression deepened in the 1930s, White River Valley farmers found it difficult to sell their crops. The large size of most Japanese American farm families virtually guaranteed hard times. Natsuhara's store, which operated on credit, held worthless paper on many families in the Auburn area. In the old days most families held to the Japanese tradition of "the father's debt is the son's." While some left town when they could not pay their creditors, others sought out the Natsuharas years later in internment camps and "laid some money down." Long after World War II, when Frank Natsuhara had taken over the management of his parents' store, periodically he received visits from the sons of Auburn farmers seeking to make good on the family's debt.

"Boy you're bringing back bad, bad memories," Frank warned, in response to a question about the weeks leading up to evacuation and internment. "Most people don't know what we went through." But local newspapers suggested the depth of animosity toward the Japanese community after the attack on Pearl Harbor. Branches of the Veterans of Foreign Wars and the American Legion in the White River Valley were extremely xenophobic and biased against anyone of Japanese ancestry.[15] They favored the evacuation of all Japanese "aliens," including their children, who were American citizens.

Rumors in the weeks that led up to the 1942 harvest ran from hot to cold, from the terror of immediate evacuation to the hope that Japanese farmers would be allowed to stay until their crops could be brought in.[16] The evacuation orders finally came at the end of May. Kiyo Maekawa vividly recalled that: "Everything was ready to be harvested. Peas were ready to be picked. Strawberries were turning color." In the prevailing atmosphere of urgency, the Maekawas' farm was sublet on short notice.

At the end of May 1942, Auburn High School held an early graduation ceremony for seniors of Japanese ancestry.[17] The Natsuhara family "sold as much as we could and we just locked the front door and gave (our kind neighbor) C. R. Sonnemann the key. He took us to the station," out of empathy with the plight of the Japanese, having personally endured rabid anti-German sentiment during the First World War. White River Valley residents of Japanese descent were sent to Pinedale, California, near Fresno. Within two months they were transferred to the Tule Lake relocation camp, where daily temperatures soared over 100° F. Two of Frank and Shizuko's daughters were born in camp. Their first child was born at Pinedale, and their second child at Tule Lake.

Photos from the period, probably taken by Mr. Sonnemann, suggest that the Natsuharas' store sign was taken down to avoid the store becoming the target of anti-Japanese hostility. Other than brief snapshots of the store intended to reassure the Natsuharas that their property was secure, there was no photographic documentation of their lives during the war years. Or so Frank generally led others to believe. Widely known as a camera buff, particularly from his work on the high school yearbook, Frank believed that the authorities would notice if he failed to turn in his equipment when cameras, radios, guns, and other things labeled as contraband were confiscated. So he allowed the sheriff's office to confiscate his box camera, which fifty years later still bore the tags that had marked it as contraband. But he only did so to evade scrutiny. In fact, he smuggled another camera into camp.

The Natsuhara children eventually left the internment camp for the U.S. Army, college, or other government approved places away from the West Coast. Chiyokichi, Sen, and daughter May remained in camp until the war ended in 1945. Although the Sonnemanns had protected the Natsuharas' store during the war to the best of their abilities, a fair amount of work was required to make the place habitable during resettlement, since the residential portion had been vandalized. The living room had been destroyed, and many furnishings had been broken.[18] So too, a poorly timed decision to sell a substantial portion of the Christopher property in the closing days of the war left the family with a terrible sense of loss and betrayal.[19]

It proved difficult for the Natsuhara family to reestablish the store because suppliers wouldn't provide them with many goods. Such suppliers based their post-war quotas on how many tons store owners had purchased in prior years, when the Natsuharas and other Japanese Americans were locked away in internment camps. Additionally, much of the Natsuharas' agricultural customer base had eroded as many Auburn born-and-raised Japanese did not return to the area. According to one source, less than twenty percent came back in the postwar period.

Years passed before many Japanese community institutions were reestablished at a level of activity even remotely comparable to their pre-war vitality, and issues of ethnic identity were complicated during this period. After their efforts to prove their patriotism and loyalty had garnered so little respect, Japanese Americans entered the era of assimilation in the 1950s on uneasy terms with their cultural heritage.

In the 1950s, eldest son Frank took over general management of the family store, changing its name from C. Natsuhara & Sons to Natsuhara's Oriental Imports and remodeling the façade of the building. He intended to mask the old false-front architecture associated with early town settlement

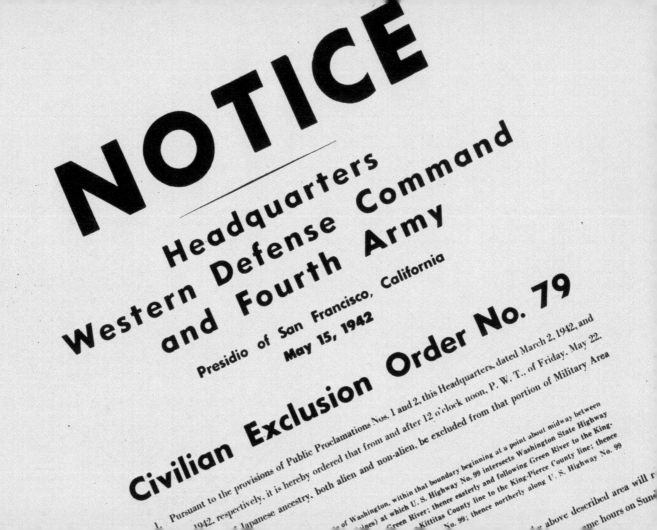

NOTICE

Headquarters
Western Defense Command
and Fourth Army

Presidio of San Francisco, California
May 15, 1942

Civilian Exclusion Order No. 79

1. Pursuant to the provisions of Public Proclamations Nos. 1 and 2, this Headquarters, dated March 2, 1942, and 1942, respectively, it is hereby ordered that from and after 12 o'clock noon, P. W. T., of Friday, May 22, of Japanese ancestry, both alien and non-alien, be excluded from that portion of Military Area

of Washington, within that boundary beginning at a point about midway between ines) at which U. S. Highway No. 99 intersects Washington State Highway Green River; thence easterly and following Green River to the King-Kittitas County line to the King-Pierce County line; thence No. 99; thence northerly along U. S. Highway No. 99

above described area will r ame hours on Sun

29
DEC

Officials
confiscating radios
and cameras in Seattle, 1941.

and introduce a fresh Oriental look to attract new customers to the gift shop.[20] Ironically, the same building that originally downplayed signs of ethnicity eventually would exaggerate them after remodeling. Chiyokichi and Sen had earlier moved to Christopher with some of their children. Frank's family spread out upstairs at the Auburn store.[21]

Over the years, Frank tended his photo albums as though they were gardens, artfully reconstructing the high school basketball team's most important plays by arranging cutouts of the players; silhouetting loved ones with heart-shaped frames; and decorating his parade of acquaintances in varied leaf shapes. Had his life and family responsibilities not been narrowly constricted by working in the family business, he would have liked to pursue his interest in photography more seriously. He did take some satisfaction in the generous access to film he had as the son of a store owner; the volume of photographs he took over the years suggests that the camera was his near-constant companion. He also was an avid collector of American and Japanese postage stamps. Well-regarded as a keeper of community memory, he could punctuate stories about the Japanese American experience with many of the old items he had saved: his box camera, strawberry crates, a 1915 catalogue from the Furuya Company, or the massive but delicately painted safe from C. Natsuhara & Sons.

Maryo, Frank Natsuhara's sister.

When Frank Natsuhara died on April 6, 1999, an era also drew to an end as the store closed. More than 300 people attended memorial services at the White River Buddhist Church, testimony to the richness of a life lived well in one place. After cremation, his remains were buried in the Natsuhara family plot at Pioneer Cemetery in Auburn, which Frank had tended, like his father before him.[22] Four months later the store burned in an arson-related fire, destroying the building and the extraordinary collection of artifacts Frank had preserved over the years.

By the time the fire died down, almost nothing remained: the massive safe; the wreckage of a well-used typewriter; a barely recognizable section of the building frame; the car Frank had driven weekly to Seattle to pick up fresh tofu, dented by falling timbers and licked clean of paint; and a lone colorful object: the ochre of a patchwork quilt, sooty and wet. There was the gruesome sight of an entire file cabinet incinerated, one drawer yawning open, revealing its scorched contents.

Though Frank Natsuhara has passed away and arson brought an end to the possibility of the store becoming a historic landmark, it is still possible to honor the Natsuharas' memory by telling their story and working to protect the remaining landmarks of Nikkei heritage.

Chapter 4

NIPPON KAN HALL

628 South Washington Street / **Seattle** / Washington

Since they didn't own a car in the years before World War II, the Inouye family walked the one mile to Nippon Kan Hall when their daughter was scheduled to appear on the engeikai (entertainment program.)

As Tama (Inouye) Tokuda later recalled:

Whatever we were going to wear that night would be wrapped up in these squares of cotton material all tied up. My mother would carry it. Usually if it was a long program, my mother would make a lunch so that we could snack while we were watching, so that was kind of fun.[1]

Attending Nippon Kan was accompanied by a measure of excitement, either due to stage fright as a performer or eager anticipation of catching up with extended family, friends, and neighbors in the audience. As community members filtered into the theater, they rented cushions to pad the wooden folding chairs. Tama Tokuda's memory is that admission was collected in the form of hana (gratuities) for many programs:

Everybody would take envelopes. I take it for granted that it was a custom that came from Japan. We gave our envelope and they recorded the name and donation in a ledger. On a great big sheet they would write in Sumi the donor's name and double the amount given them and it would be hung on the wall. By the time the program started, the whole north wall would be covered.[2]

While the audience settled into their seats, the performers would finish getting dressed and applying makeup. This preparation took place in the basement, since the theater lacked space backstage. Recalling the layout, Tama Tokuda pointed out that:

There really is nothing behind [the Nippon Kan stage]. All the dressing rooms and the makeup rooms were below. The first level below there was a long mirror so that actors could apply their makeup. In our case, the teacher always made up our faces. Then, if you went one level below, that's where we got dressed in our costumes. [In one corner] they had some food so people could munch. And in another corner was a photographer. He would have a camera set up. After we got dressed we would have pictures taken, for our keepsake.[3]

Upstairs, the audience was "socializing and waiting, clapping hopefully for the curtain to open up." Lessons with Mrs. Nakamura, who "was a tiny lady, not even five feet tall," prepared young Tama Inouye to perform classical Japanese dances on the stage of Nippon Kan. No amount of rehearsal quelled the anxiety of waiting her turn to go onstage. Tama recalled:

As a child, you know how nervous you get. While we're getting dressed you can hear the chairs shifting and the clapping. To this day it makes me nervous to remember your number is getting closer and closer.

Performing before such an audience had a special intimacy, since it was filled with familiar faces, although Tama, for one, doesn't remember "ever seeing the people in the audience" from up on stage, since she "wasn't that relaxed." With the drawing of the curtains, which were hand-pulled with counterweights, the performance would begin. Although she last appeared on the program at Nippon Kan in October, 1941, only a few months before the bombing of Pearl Harbor, when interviewed in May of 1997 Tama Tokuda recalled the sensation of coming on stage as though it were yesterday:

Interior of Nippon Kan Hall, 1998.

Meeting of the Japanese Association at Nippon Kan Hall. Original advertisements on curtain.

A man pulls the curtains from side to side. And while he opens it, they always have [another] man [who] uses wooden clackers — two sticks about 8 or 10 inches — you clack the two together and it makes this very sharp sound. As the curtain is pulled, the tempo gets faster and faster. Every performance was ushered in with that sound. It still thrills me when I hear that sound.

Traditional performances of kabuki or Japanese dance might occupy an evening program. Budd Fukei described the stage on these occasions:

Upstage on the left were the drummers, and on the extreme right were the shamisen [lute] players. On the extreme left was the hanamichi [runway] leading to the stage, which was built of wood. The ceiling was very high, so high, in fact, that the acoustics were not acoustics by any stretch of the imagination. The sounds bounced off in every direction.[4]

It was not unusual for there to be many numbers when the program was organized by local dancing and singing schools, as Tama Tokuda later explained.

There were a lot of programs that went on in the Nippon Kan. Quite a few teachers taught at that time and they all had their own recitals.

The time intervals between amateur numbers tended to go on a little too long, however, and the waiting nearly "drove us crazy." Impatient children ran up and down the stairs between the main floor and the balcony during these extended intermissions, while adults caught up with relatives and neighbors. Soon the familiar clapping of wooden sticks and opening of the curtain quieted the audience, and the creaking of the wooden chairs ceased, signaling that the next performance was beginning.[5] Family members nudged one another — with discreet whispers and pointed fingers — as familiar faces appeared onstage. The Issei delighted in being transported back to their homeland, if only for a brief interlude.

After the performance, families began the walk home, savoring the experience for as long as possible. As Tama Tokuda recalls:

I still enjoy looking at the old costumes my mother sewed for my dance roles. Once, after I had become a mother myself, I asked her "why did you sacrifice so much to give me those dance lessons and costumes?" She said, "it was the light of my life." Then I realized how lonesome she must have been for the culture she had left behind, coming to this strange country. All those programs at Nippon Kan must have been a great source of comfort to the Issei in our community.

Nippon Kan loomed large in the memory of Minoru Masuda, who eventually became a professor of psychiatry and behavioral sciences at the University of Washington:

If that darkened hall could speak, what a flood of recollections it could call forth. For me, I can hear the thunderclap of sticks heralding the opening of the maku [curtain]; I can see the banners of money contributions displayed and strung on the north wall; I can recall the dramatic voice of the Kabuki actor striding down the hanamichi [stage extension]; I can hear the twang of the shamisen and the intonation of the storyteller; and I can feel once again the excitement and the hubbub. Later, as we ourselves became the actors, we knew butterflies in the stomach and stage fright, experienced the glare of the footlights, and knew the chaos of the dressing room.[6]

"One needs to know the solidarity and social isolation of the Japanese community to appreciate what the Nippon Kan meant to it. It was, in reality, the hub of the Nihonmachi world and its peoples."

MINORU MASUDA

AUDIENCE MEMBER, NIPPON KAN HALL

Lotus Entertainment, circa 1930.

Construction of Seattle's Nippon Kan Hall, located at Washington and Maynard, started in 1907 and was completed several years later. It was intended to serve as a social and cultural hall for Seattle's Nikkei community. Early plans to house a language school within the community building were abandoned in favor of the combination hotel and clubhouse, which initially was intended to accommodate an influx of Japanese tourists in conjunction with the 1909 Alaska-Yukon-Pacific Exposition. However, it was not completed in time to profit from the event.[7]

Reporting on early plans for Nippon Kan, Seattle's daily newspapers identified the model for this building "as an American club house, though not as expensive as the more pretentious homes of the Seattle clubs."[8] In some sense this description was accurate, since the building was intended to serve as an umbrella for many community organizations. As built, it constituted a hybrid type that served not only as a workingmen's hotel, but also as a theatre and community hall for Seattle's Japanese immigrants and their children. As architectural historian David Rash wrote, "The building incorporated clubrooms and dormitories for young men in the upper floors, an auditorium with stage to be the home venue of three locally based theatrical troupes on the principal floor, and the almost obligatory retail storefronts at street level."[9]

Left, Nippon Kan Hall. Above, the entrance after remodeling.

Performance at the Nippon Kan Hall, circa 1915-20.

The three-and-a-half-story brick building, overlooking Seattle's Nihonmachi, was constructed by the Cascade Investment Company, a subsidiary of the Oriental Trading Company which was devoted to real estate development.[10] According to David Rash, it was the first of many structures in Seattle's International District to be designed by the architectural firm of Thompson and Thompson.[11] The exterior lacked any distinctively Japanese architectural features, other than the mix of residential, commercial, and civic uses typical of buildings in urban Nihonmachi. Seattle resident Budd Fukei's description of Nippon Kan's entry suggests that it was designed to blend into the urban fabric rather than call attention to itself: "Nippon Kan was located in a hotel building, its unpretentious doorway was between the hotel entrance and the door to a grocery store. Inside, Nippon Kan was equally informal."[12]

The construction of the Nippon Kan was contemporaneous with the Japanese Building at the Alaska-Yukon-Pacific Exposition as well as with the Seattle Buddhist Temple, which suggests that more exotic or at least more expressive models of ethnic and national identity were available as architectural alternatives but were actively rejected for the design of this community building. Then again, the relatively neutral facade may have helped to mark Nippon Kan as a civic space with the potential to transcend many of the lines of cleavage that organized the Japanese immigrant community and which had the potential to divide it by class, religion, and prefectural origin, among other factors.

There are also some indications that theatres in Japan were not particularly expressive in façade treatments. Terry's *Guide to the Japanese Empire* (1927) suggests that theatre structures "often occupy mean sites in side streets and with few exceptions are devoid of architectural charm."[13] Yet their interiors were designed to support dramatic traditions distinctively Japanese in character.

The peculiar lateral aisles which project from the side of the stage [butai] are called hanamichi [flowery way], and are used by the actors [yakusha] and actresses [onnayakusha] in approaching or leaving it. The stage usually rests upon rollers, like a railway turntable, and when a new scene is wanted it is turned round with the scenery and actors in position. The latter sometimes speak their parts [often in strained and hoarse, apoplectic voices]; at other times they posture and make pantomimic gestures which are interpreted by the chorus accompanied by samisen.

The façade of the Nippon Kan building was relatively unadorned. However, the exterior presented a striking contrast with the space inside. Crossing the threshold took Japanese immigrants into a vibrant cultural space. Nippon Kan became a center for community gatherings at a time when, as Miyoshi Yorita recalled, "the only [other] entertainment facilities in Japanese town were movie theaters [such as the Atlas]."[14] Gensaburo Ohashi recalled that there were four Japanese theatrical groups in Seattle:

Seattle Drama Circle [kabuki], Jiyu Gekidan [modern], Azumadan and Futabakai [modern]. Later the Gigei Club was established, to which I belonged, and it was renamed Geijutsu Kyokai. We featured kabuki. Actors were all amateurs, except Sojin Kamiyama, a professional in Hollywood movies who once belonged to Jiyu Gekidan. Each group had about 15 members of various occupations... businessmen, gardeners, restaurant owners, railroad workers, and so on. Our final rehearsals were at Japanese Hall...we had two days' break before performance. Performance[s] were held on Saturdays and Sundays... twice a month. We always had something to perform each month. Admission was 75c at most. Fukiyosekai gave free performances but set a box at the entrance for contributions to pay off the rent of the hall.[15]

Reflecting on the value of this cultural work to the Nikkei, Gensaburo Ohashi told historian Kazuo Ito,

To the life of the Japanese community, which had very little other enter-tainment in those days, we must have made an important contribution.[16]

Nippon Kan hosted numerous types of performances, from the traditional forms of entertainment favored by the Issei, who were lonesome for the land they had left behind, to the American styles favored by Nisei youth — harmonica and big band performances. Nippon Kan Hall also was the site of vigorous political debates; innumerable fundraisers, such as those for the championship-winning Taiyo baseball club; and traditional cultural practices, such as the annual ceremony marking the Japanese Emperor's birthday. It also was a favorite venue for wedding parties. The transitory and flexible nature of the space could accommodate the full range of expressions of ethnic identity, from the Issei's powerful displays of nationalist sentiment, to the Nisei's preoccupation with distinc-tively American entertainment forms.

But the theater was fundamentally an Issei institution and, as such, it was designed with at least one traditional architectural element required for Japanese drama. The stage was built with a small exten-sion, the hanamichi, that was an essential element in kabuki theater, as Tama Tokuda recalled:

At the juncture where the stage met that runway, there was a little percussion area [with] drums and cymbals and different sound effects. So they would accompany any movement that was [happening] on the stage. The runway was actually used for dramatic highlights and grand entrances and grand exits. It's really a very nice kabuki touch.[17]

The enactment of traditional dramatic practices in the theatre trans-formed Nippon Kan Hall into a distinctively Japanese space, at least for the duration of the performance.

Issei took great pleasure in the performances of ancient Japanese plays; shamisen and shakuhachi (bamboo flute) players; and the classical odori dances, which allowed the Nikkei to engage as performers as well as spectators. Traditional values such as filial piety were often reinforced as dramatic themes, reflecting the Issei's hope that some Japanese values would be absorbed by their children.

Dance, drama, and other entertainments were performed at Japanese Hall. Besides Sesshu [Sessue] Hayakawa and Sojin Kamiyama, then movie actors in Hollywood, well-known singers like Tamaki Miura, Toshiko Sekiya, and Yoshie Fujiwara came from Japan to perform. And even local talents gave rokyoku shows. So people could forget that they were living so far from home.[18]

In a fictionalized account of her experiences attending events at Nippon Kan Hall, Monica Sone ably painted a portrait of the intergenera-tional conflicts that could arise when Issei and Nisei both occupied the space. Unlike Tama Tokuda, who found much satisfaction in learning the art, Monica Sone was horrified by the degree of restraint she witnessed at her first classical dance recital. What others surely viewed as graceful movement, Sone interpreted as female powerlessness and confinement.

I saw a small girl standing as motionless as a statue in the center of the stage, her back turned to the audience. Her wide sash of glittering old brocade was tied into an elaborate butterfly bow. Suddenly, a chorus of women's voices, which sounded as if it were being strained through a

Nippon Kan Hall was a favorite venue for wedding parties.

Down the hall from a space occupied by a weekly meeting of the Dharma Exchange, past rooms which were used by a government agency during the internment years, there is a room in the basement of the Seattle Buddhist Temple brimming with old props and costumes. Opening the door to this room is a shock to the senses because of the sheer number of objects that evoke the shibai and kabuki performances of the interwar period. There Japanese wigs dangle like fish from a wire. A rare box of stage makeup once owned by featured performer Kiki Hagimori, who was affiliated with the Buddhist Temple's theater troupe, Lotus Entertainment, hints at the dramatic transformation in appearances that were achieved in Nippon Kan's dressing rooms prior to each show. Trunks are neatly packed with layers of kimono, some real and others good enough to pass for real when worn by minor characters and viewed from a distance. Soldiers' helmets and makeshift swords once used in military dramas now stand down. These and hundreds of other rare artifacts were saved by the Archives Committee of the Seattle Buddhist Temple when the Geijitsukyokai drama club, organized in 1920, finally disbanded.

GEIJITSUKYOKAI MEMORIES

NIPPON KAN HALL Seattle / Washington [78]

Nippon Kan Hall, 1998

sieve, drifted out from offstage, accompanied by the plucking of samisens…
The singing sounded alarmingly like growling, moans and strangulation.
Then the girl turned slowly around.

Her face was masked in deathly white rice powder, with jet black eyes
and eyebrows, and a tiny red dot of a mouth. On her head, she wore a
huge, black pompadour wig, decorated with bright, glittering hair orna-
ments. Her rich purple kimono was patterned with gorgeous golden
chrysanthemums. I waited for her to start dancing… that is, to leap and
whirl and get going, but all I saw were undulating, butter-soft hands, a
slight tremor of the head, and a delicate foot stamp which could hardly
have hurt an ant. During the entire performance, the dancer did not
cover more than a few square inches. And she never smiled.[19]

Similarly, the annual celebration of the Meiji Emperor's birthday
required a level of patriotic feeling mostly lost on the Nisei, who felt trapped
by Issei rituals that meant little to them. As Monica Sone recalled:

Once a year when spring rolled around, sensei made the announcement:
'Tomorrow there'll be no school because it's Tenchosetsu. We'll meet at
Nippon Kan Hall at 2 pm. I'll be taking roll call there.' I groaned. I thought
it was wasteful to spend a beautiful spring afternoon crowded into a dingy,
crumbling hall and sit numbly through a ritual that never varied one word
or gesture from year to year. But I knew there was no escape.[20]

Japanese and Western etiquette tended to come into conflict at just
these sorts of high-stakes public events. The fact that they were largely
closed to outsiders may have made it possible to display tensions within
the Japanese American community that would have been suppressed

in the presence of the hakujin (Caucasians.) In Monica Sone's fictionalized account, the high school girls' attempt to come to the event dressed
in their best spring bonnets deeply offends the principal of the language
school, who considers it "an insult to the Emperor that you should keep
your hats on."[21] The evidence suggests that Nippon Kan accommodated
rituals of ethnic solidarity while also serving as a powerful backdrop for
the drama of emerging differences in cultural identity across generations
of Japanese Americans.

Like other Nihonmachi institutions, Nippon Kan closed soon after
the Japanese attack on Pearl Harbor. The FBI must have kept a close
watch on this key community institution in the final weeks leading up to
mass evacuation and internment of Japanese Americans. In January
1942, authorities entered Nippon Kan Hall while a movie was being shown
and demanded that specific Issei in the audience report to the theatre
office. Witnesses recall that a message was projected onto the movie screen:
"Mr. X, report to the office," whereupon those singled out were arrested.
How officials knew who would be in attendance remains a subject of
speculation more than sixty years later.

While many Nikkei institutions were revived in the postwar period
— albeit in diminished or altered form — and the Astor Hotel was reopened, the Nippon Kan remained dark for nearly forty years until architect
Edward Burke and others restored the theatre in 1980 and secured its
listing on the National Register of Historic Places, reviving its use as a community cultural hall.[22] With the help of Nippon Kan Heritage Association,
the landmark building now owned by the Stroum family has been brought
back to life, blending its traditional function as a cultural hearth for Seattle's
Nihonmachi with its broader use as a performance venue. Many original
interior details remain, from rosette lights to backstage grafitti. It is under
consideration for National Historic Landmark status.

Chapter 5

HASHIDATE-YU

302 Sixth Avenue South / **Seattle** / Washington

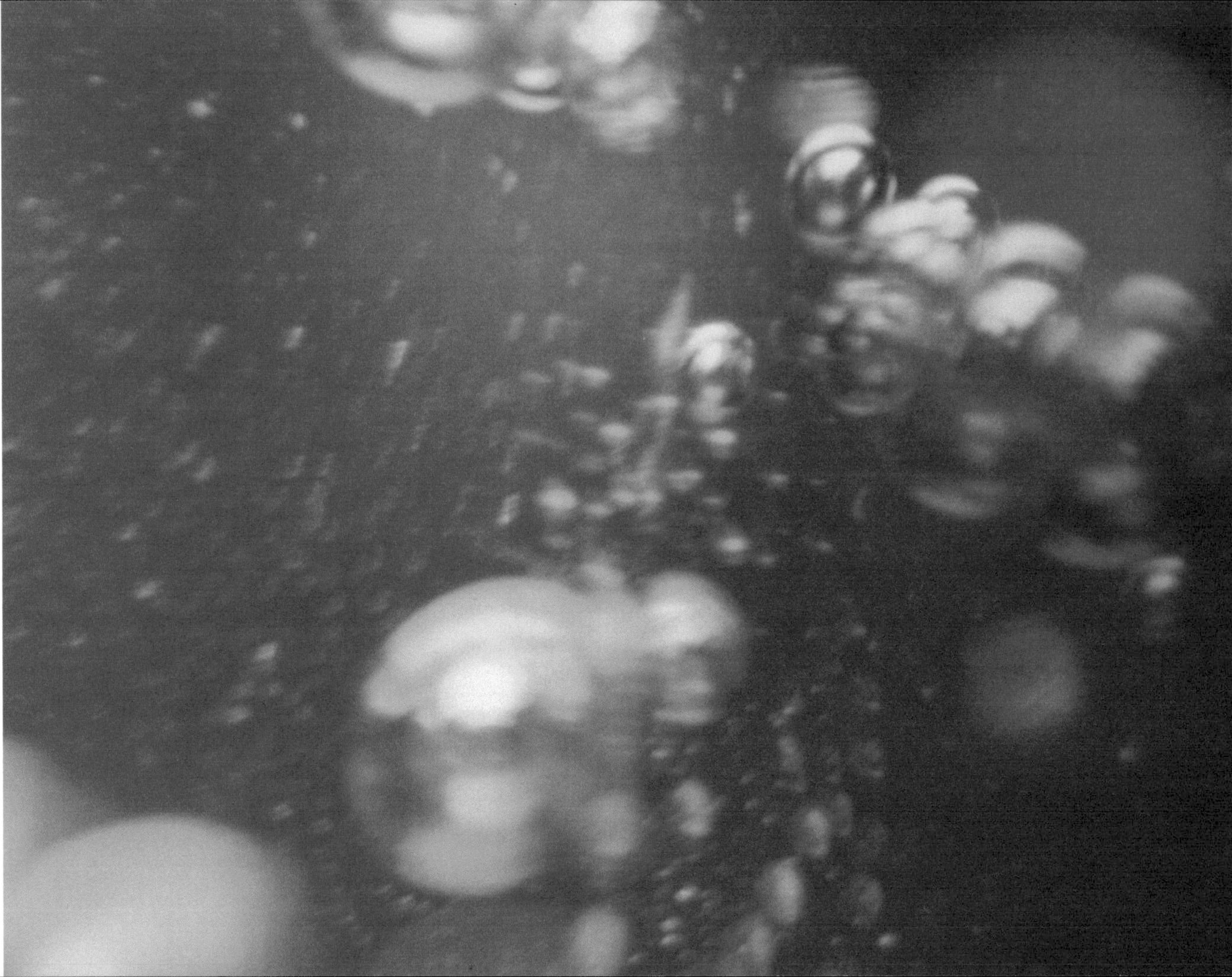

When Ed Sano descended several steps into the basement of the Panama Hotel in 1999 and passed
through the double doors that once marked Hashidate-Yu, he entered a place that had been closed
for more than thirty years, since his mother, Shigeko, and father, Fukuo Sano, retired from operating
the last Japanese bathhouse in Seattle. Though no longer operational, Hashidate-Yu is one of only
two historic sento (public bathhouses) that are known to have survived in the United States, where
hundreds once flourished in Japanese American communities. Benign neglect for two decades
combined with careful stewardship in recent years has left Hashidate-Yu in remarkably good condition, with surviving details that serve as poignant reminders of daily life in Nihonmachi (Japantowns)
before World War II.

　　While a return visit to Hashidate-Yu was somewhat unsettling for Ed Sano, since work in the
family bathhouse and laundry business occupied such a large part of his youth, former patrons
who have come to look around typically delight in vivid memories of soaking in the super-heated
ofuro (soaking tub) as it was an extremely relaxing and pleasurable social activity. Elderly women
usually giggle at their first glimpse of the men's section, which they had never seen during scores
of visits during the 1930s, when men and women occupied separate sections of the facility. Elderly
men, upon seeing the women's section for the first time (or, in some cases, for the first time as
adults as all children typically bathed with their mothers), usually are surprised by its relatively small
size compared with the men's section – as though silently registering the unequal status of women
that was an accepted feature of Issei life in those years.

Hashidate-Yu operated out of the basement of the Panama Hotel, a single room occupancy (SRO) hotel in what is now known as Seattle's International District, for more than 50 years — from 1910 until the mid-1960s — closing only during the evacuation and relocation period associated with Japanese internment during the Second World War. All indications are that the bathhouse was built at the time of the hotel's construction in 1910 by the first Japanese architect to practice in the city, Saburo Ozasa. The location of Hashidate-Yu bathhouse at Sixth and South Main put it at the heart of Seattle's Nihonmachi, which served as a regional draw for Japanese immigrants who had settled on the urban periphery, as well as a residential center in its own right.

Immigrants came to soak at the sento because life was hard, hot water was relaxing, bathing facilities were scarce in prewar housing, and it was a traditional cultural activity. Japanese bathing traditions are at least twelve centuries old and have taken many forms. Bathhouses have existed in Japan since the eighth century, when they were a central feature of Buddhist temples. The earliest public bathhouses were connected with temples and monasteries, such as the one in the Second Month Hall of the Todai-Ji Temple in Nara. Built on a natural spring, the temple served as a bathhouse for the monks as well as a site of Buddhist purification rites.

Buddhist temples provided baths as resources for the general public, who lacked private facilities.[1] Although its religious connotations eventually faded, the act of bathing persisted in Japan. Bathhouses became social gathering places for urban dwellers. The first sento was established in Osaka in 1590; and by the mid 1800s there were 550 bathhouses in Tokyo alone. Neighborhood bathhouses in the eighteenth century were often two-story structures, with rooms on the second level for relaxing, chatting, eating, drinking, and playing games.

Natural bathing facilities such as hot springs (onsen) have been highly valued by Japanese for their healing capabilities. Bathing is still a valued tradition in Japan and was among the most significant traditional cultural practices to be brought over to the United States by the first Japanese immigrants. Ofuro (soaking tubs) that Issei constructed in American Nihonmachi are among the few surviving elements of the built environment that reflect a distinctively Japanese American heritage.

Several Japanese bathhouses were located within Seattle's Nihonmachi. Those who lived outside of the city frequently would visit Japantown on the weekend to do shopping and attend events at community landmarks such as Nippon Kan Hall. Seattle hotel owner Ritoji Nishimura,

Natural bathing facilities are highly valued by the Japanese for their healing capabilities. At right, the women's bath at Makiba-no-ie Ryokan in Yufuin, Japan, 2000.

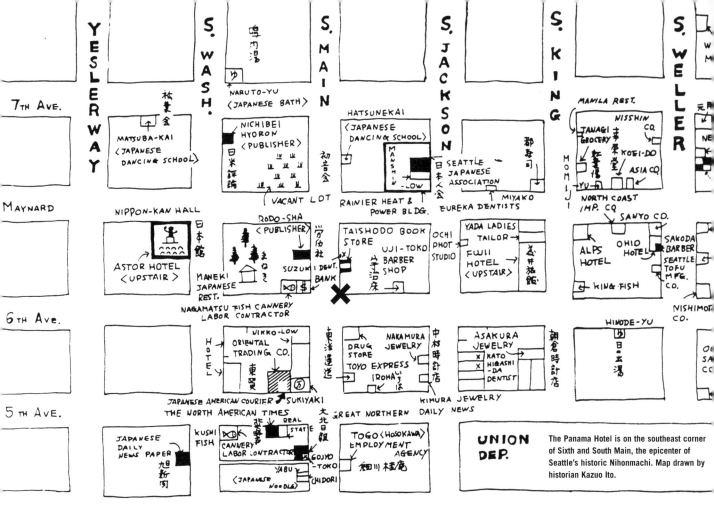

The Panama Hotel is on the southeast corner of Sixth and South Main, the epicenter of Seattle's historic Nihonmachi. Map drawn by historian Kazuo Ito.

born in Ehime Prefecture in 1878, began work for an Italian farmer in the South Park area (just outside of Seattle) in 1903. An agricultural worker, engaged in backbreaking labor, he would make the half hour trek to Seattle's Nihonmachi, where he would enjoy the many services, including the Japanese public bath on South Main Street.[2] These establishments likewise provided the only bathing facilities for Nihonmachi residents who lived in storefront businesses, hotels, and rooming houses in the pre-World War II period. Nisei children in those few prewar households with a private bath envied their neighbors' trip to the sento, although viewed purely in economic terms, those with private tubs were more privileged. Former patron Dell Uchida recalls the prominence of bathhouses throughout the community as well as a particular fondness for Hashidate-Yu:

There were about four bathhouses [in Seattle's Nihonmachi] that I remember: the Shimoji, the Hinode, the Naruto, owned by the Kosugis on Washington, and the Hashidate under the Panama Hotel… The area was almost solid Japanese who mostly lived in housekeeping rooms with just a toilet. There were at least 10 bathhouses in the '20s and '30s in Nihonmachi or Japantown.

We lived in one room behind my dad's dye works business on James Street, and we didn't have a tub; so Papa used to take us to the furo at least once a week… we went mostly to the Hashidate. My dad drove my brother and me about 8 blocks to 6th and Main in his 1926 Whippet. We entered the Hashidate Bath House off 6th Avenue and went down the stairs into the office lobby… Now I realize how good the baths were. I just took it for granted in those days. We usually went on Sundays. After the bath, we sometimes went to the Chanbara [Samurai movies] at the old Atlas Theater just down the hill… They had these comic cartoons in between. We loved that.[3]

One of the most important things that set soaking in Japanese ofuro apart from typical Western bathing practices is the etiquette of cleaning the body before entering the bath. Typical bathhouses required that patrons shower or scrub using water from a wash basin and provided a taoru (towel) and tenugui (hand wiper), soap, shampoo, and other sanitary items. The practices employed at Hashidate-Yu, described here by Ed Sano, closely parallel traditional practices in Japan, with the exception of the mixed-sex bathing that prevailed before contact with the West:

An early advertisement for the Panama Hotel.

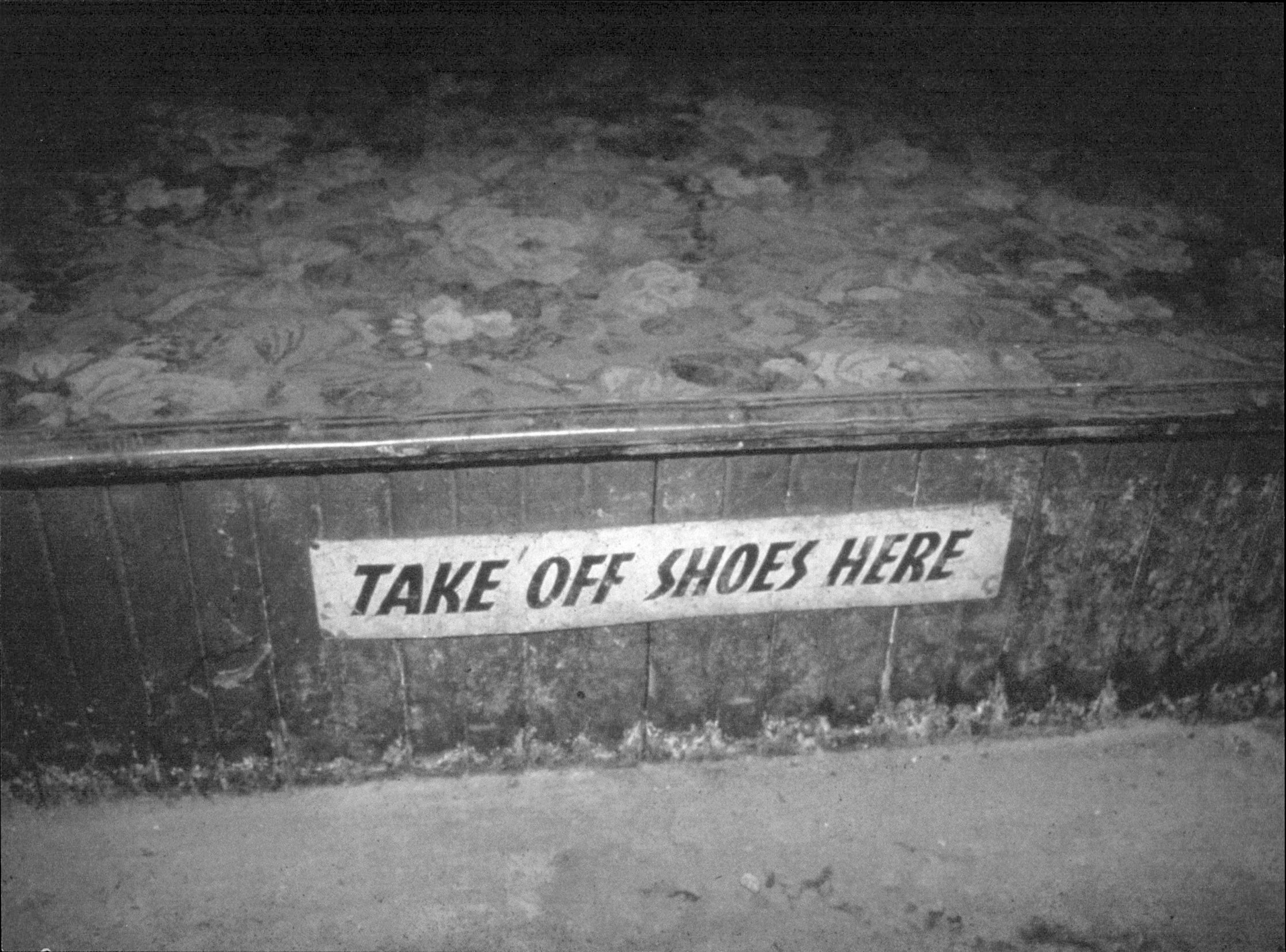
TAKE OFF SHOES HERE

The sensual pleasures of warmth and cleanliness seem to bring out the best in people: the Japanese respond with happy chatter and contented sighs. The smooth floors and walls of tile magnify the din of spirited conversation punctuated by splashes and the high-pitched laughter of children. The sounds of the bathhouse change with the shifting cycle of the daily clock, beginning relatively quietly in the midafternoon, when the doors open to the first customers – generally, elderly

PLEASURES

retired folk eager for the company of other senior citizens. Later in the afternoon, the decibel level rises as the bathhouse fills up with children home from school and young mothers bathing babies before going home to begin preparing the evening meal. The noise reaches its highest pitch during the evening hours when older children come for their baths, along with fathers and young single men and women, many of whom may have thrown back a drink or two on their way to the bathhouse. By ten-thirty or eleven at night, quiet begins to fall on the bathhouse again as weary shopkeepers or late-returning office workers enjoy a relaxing soak before drifting home to bed. The last sounds of the day are the gurgle of drains, the splashing of water, and the swishing of soapy brushes as the proprietors and staff scrub the floors and tubs and rinse away the aftermath of one long day and prepare the bathhouse for the next.

Women's tub
at Hashidate-Yu

OF THE JAPANESE BATH

by Peter Grilli and Dana Levy

Men's tub
at Hashidate-Yu

Well, you were supposed to wash up outside [the tub], then you got these pans, washbasins, so you'd get that, the soap, a regular wash towel and a bath towel. You'd leave your bath towel back up there where the locker was. You'd take the wash towel and wash yourself with that. You were supposed to wash, and then get this bath water and wash all the soap off, and then you'd jump in [the tub]... And then you'd soak.[4]

Former Hashidate-Yu patron Dell Uchida fondly remembered the bathing protocol that was essential to the overall experience:

[In the bathhouse lobby] we paid 35 cents each and they gave us a towel... Then, we went into the steamy furo room. We changed in this one room in the far corner; it was nice and had a rug. We never had to take anything along because they supplied everything. Next, we went into the men's or women's side and stood on the raised wooden floor boards next to the soaking tubs. We wet ourselves with a tenugui (a long, narrow piece of simple cotton) cloth and soaped ourselves; then, used a loofah like scrubber. We scooped water from the big tub with a bucket to rinse ourselves off and we were ready for our soak.[5]

A high standard of personal hygiene was expected from all patrons, including prewashing and prohibiting body fluids from entering the tub. Mas Fukuhara describes the protocol at the baths:

Although there were no written rules, everyone was expected to abide by common sense bathing etiquette such as thoroughly washing and rinsing before entering the tub and to refrain from passing gas or polluting the bath water with any objects or bodily fluids except perspiration. Of course, there were always a few people who ignored one or more of the unwritten rules of good bathing conduct.[6]

Preparing the bath water was one of Ed Sano's daily responsibilities, and his return visit sparked long-forgotten memories of the usual morning ritual, which was focused on achieving the perfect bath water temperature. At ten in the morning, when the bathhouse opened,

Mr. Fukuo Sano

You got to start the boiler to get the water hot for everything, laundry and the bath house. The hot water naturally goes to the top, [but] the cold water's down. So we used to have a big 1 x 6 board, ten feet long, [that] we'd use to turn and mix the water. Otherwise it would be really hot and you couldn't hardly stick your hand in there. But when you mixed it up it was just about right. [7]

Ed Sano's morning routine did not go unnoticed by sento patrons. Some users recall the combination of pleasure and pain when entering the bath, considering the intense heat of the water:

The first patrons of the day always encountered a tub, which sat heating all day with the temperature stratified and seemingly hot enough on the surface to boil eggs. It was a ritual for the first man in to run cold water and mix the bath water. Most of us youngsters couldn't take the heat so we turned on the cold water full bore and even then slithered into the tub right next to the cold water spigot. But to preserve some machismo, we lied about how good it was as we gritted our teeth and endured bath temperatures in excess of what we considered comfortable. Looking every bit like boiled lobsters (probably more like boiled shrimp) we grabbed our towels, dried ourselves, ordered an ice cold soda pop and relaxed on benches and seats in a space north of the locker room. For many Nisei, sipping an ice cold pop after a parboiling in the Japanese bath was close to ecstasy and ranks near the top of their blissful childhood memories. [8]

Sento and Nisei baseball fit hand-in-glove during the pre-war years, as Ed Sano recalled:

Especially after the game most of them would come down to the bathhouse before they go home, right after the game. They'd soak in there, I guess, to relieve their worried bones. Quite a few teams came down.[9]

Frank Natsuhara fondly recalled bringing the Auburn baseball team he managed to Hashidate-Yu. On occasions when the team played especially well, an enthusiastic fan might follow them to the sento and treat everyone to dinner afterwards. The busiest hours at Hashidate-Yu were during the evening:

Mrs. Shigeko Sano

Most folks would come after 6, after they eat, and it got busier after 8 o'clock. Most folks would come with their kids, or else the older people were more or less single, the bachelors, older people, they would come down.[10]

Many older Nisei warmly remember the variety of bathhouses that existed in western cities before World War II. Tsuneki Kagawa operated a bathhouse in Portland, Oregon, called Ebisuyu. He described the operation to historian Kazuo Ito, noting his efforts to preserve the style of a typical bathhouse in Japan:

I myself started a Japanese bath, Ebisuyu [in Portland]…There was another bath house [nearby]. They had new equipment, but mine was old and the tub was wooden. But old Issei seemed to prefer this wooden tub to the new one, so I had regular customers…The bath house was divided into two rooms, one for men and one for women, just as in Japan.[11]

Community directories published by the Nikkei press indicate the popularity of Japanese bathhouses in the pre-World War II period and suggest the other kinds of businesses with which they were associated. A directory produced by the Southern California newspaper *Rafu Shimpo* reveals a multitude of bathhouses in the state but especially concentrated in Nihonmachi of larger cities, such as Los Angeles and San Francisco.[12] In 1939 alone, there were several bathhouses in Los Angeles and San Francisco, and at least ten more scattered among the smaller towns of Palos Verdes, San Pedro, El Centro, Oxnard, Santa Barbara, Fresno, and Salinas. According to *Rafu Shimpo*, Los Angeles's Nikkei community had a choice of at least nine bathhouses in 1939, the most of which were clustered in the heart of Little Tokyo from 300-700 East First Street. They included the American Bath, Hiro Bath, Nihon-boro, and Tokiwa-Yu. No less than five barbers and three pool halls were also located on that same stretch, with many more sited on surrounding streets.

San Francisco had at least five bathhouses in operation during the prewar period. Three were located between 1600 and 1900 Post Street: Kikunoyu Bath, Minatoyu Bath, and Post Bath, surrounded by more than a dozen barbershops, while Pacific Bath and Tokyo Bath were located on Stockton and Geary Streets, respectively. The 1939 directory suggests that some bathhouses, barbershops, and pool halls were co-located, such as the Pacific Bath & Barbershop or Futatsuki

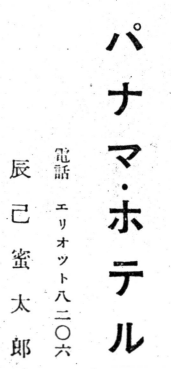

PANAMA HOTEL

605½ Main St.,
Seattle, Wash.

沙市メーン街六〇五半

パナマ・ホテル

電話 エリオット八二〇六

辰己巳蜜太郎

Nakano Painter　725 24th Ave. So.
Uchida Painter　217½ 10th Ave.

呂・靴修理・球場
Bath, Shoerepair, Pool Halls.

湯所

Hashidate, Bath　302 6th Ave. So.
Kenny's Shoe Service
　1017½ Jackson St.
New Golden Shoe Shop　619 Weller

所會所場場

Special Shoe Co.　826 Jackson St.
Yesler Shoe Shop 2021 Yesler Way
Ishida Pool Hall　502 Main St.
King Pool Hall　511 King St.

A laundry sign marked the entry to Hashidate-Yu at 302 6th Avenue South.

Barbershop & Pool Hall. Similarly, Kikunoyu Bath, Suzuki Barbershop, and Kikuno Pool Hall all operated out of 1615 Post Street, although the different names and telephone numbers suggest independent management.[13] Others enjoyed immediate adjacencies, such as Nakahara Barbershop and Hideshima Pool Hall.

Even smaller Japanese American communities, such as Salt Lake City's cluster of Japanese businesses in the vicinity of West-South Temple near West 1st and 2nd South, had multiple listings in the 1939 directory, including Igata Barber & Baths, Iyetsuka Barber & Baths, and Matsuda Pool Hall.[14] There is no evidence that customer preferences for one bathhouse over another were divided by religion, prefectural origin, or other obvious lines, though the activities of soaking in ofuro, getting a haircut, or playing pool clearly were social activities that reinforced relationship networks in the Nikkei community.

Like bathhouses, Nihonmachi laundries were typically located in the basements of buildings and functioned in combination with ground-floor barbershops and pool halls. These, in turn, depended on the presence of single room occupancy hotels, where the patrons, including many bachelors, relied on larger communities to provide basic services. Bathhouses and hand laundry operations frequently were combined because they were compatible businesses. In fact, quite frequently, the same boiler provided the water for both the baths and the laundry, and laundry facilities often washed towels used by bathhouse patrons and hotel guests.[15] Towels continually needed to be laundered for use in the bathhouse anyway, so expanded operation as a laundry meant additional income. Both were wet, steamy environments that could be collocated. Where water for the soaking tubs was heated by a boiler, as opposed to a steam company, excess heat in the boiler room could be used to dry the laundry, as was the case at Hashidate-Yu. So too, the bathhouse workday was heavily loaded in the morning and evening, leaving the middle of the day for laundry work. Finally, many bathhouses operated as family businesses, so the combined facility optimized the labor of men, women, and children and maximized family income.

This combination of businesses, located in districts with a large number of hotels and other housing with limited bathing facilities, provided essential services for the Japanese American community. The dense cluster of personal services meant customers "brought their laundry on Saturday, had a haircut and bath, put clean-washed clothes on, and left their soiled things to be

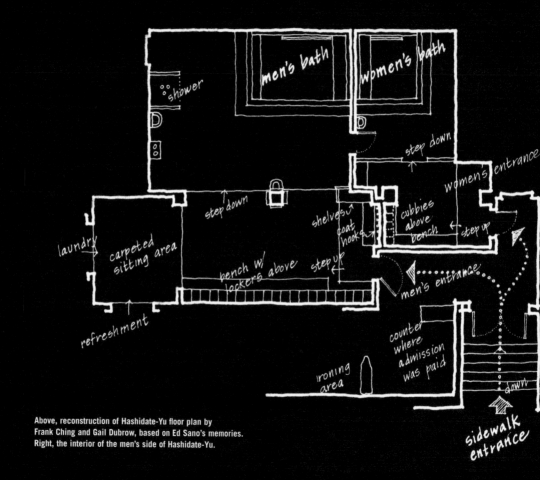

men's bath

women's bath

shower

step down

women's entrance

step down

shelves

coat hooks

cubbies above bench

step up

laundry

carpeted sitting area

bench w/ lockers above

step up

men's entrance

refreshment

counter where admission was paid

ironing area

down

sidewalk entrance

Above, reconstruction of Hashidate-Yu floor plan by
Frank Ching and Gail Dubrow, based on Ed Sano's memories.
Right, the interior of the men's side of Hashidate-Yu.

washed all in one trip."[16] This triad of services was especially in demand within the urban environment. In farming communities, women generally were responsible for providing the family services of laundry, haircutting, and preparing the baths. In urban Nihonmachi, bachelors had to look outside the traditional family structure to have these basic needs met. Even the most frugal of urban men considered spending money for a haircut and bath a necessity. The founder of the Main Fish Company, who pinched pennies to develop his store, for example, did not pay his brothers a salary in the early days of the business, giving them "nothing except money for haircuts and baths."[17]

Vancouver, British Columbia, also had a prominent Nihonmachi, which allowed new immigrants a place of transition between the old world and the new. The Nihonmachi thrived and evolved into an active Japanese American community. According to Tsutae Sato, the principal of the Vancouver B.C. Japanese Joint Language School:

There were three Japanese daily newspapers – Tairiku Nippo, Canada Shimbun and Minshu. Whites called Powell Street 'Little Tokyo.' Gradually the Japanese population increased and there came to be three Buddhist Churches. The Japanese Language School developed [had] a thousand students. The Japanese could dine on miso soup with tofu and rice with Japanese tea poured over it, accompanied by pickled radish. [They] could then console their homesick hearts while dipping leisurely in the Japanese public bath. Though they had connections with whites concerning their businesses, Japanese could live among themselves in their daily life.[18]

Clearly, Japantowns in the western United States and Canada allowed Japanese immigrants to share familiar cultural traditions and adapt to new settings. Religious institutions, Japanese language schools, laundry facilities, barbershops, and bathhouses were all places for gathering, sharing resources, networking, and affirmation of cultural traditions in a new land.

Another reason Japanese immigrants established their own services was that many anti-Japanese exclusionists reflected their prejudice through denying services to nonwhite people. Indeed, barbershops and restaurants under white management were well known for their refusal to serve Japanese immigrants, and movie theaters often refused to sell them tickets for the best seats, requiring Japanese immigrants as well as their American-born children to be seated in the balcony with African Americans. Given their own pride and prejudices, this second-class seating was infuriating. Some swimming facilities also excluded the Japanese among other people of color. The most widespread form of discrimination limited the sale and rental of real property to white people through restrictive covenants and informal agreements. For these reasons, the hotels, barbershops, restaurants, bathhouses, and Nihonmachi theaters were welcoming gathering places that insulated customers from the harsh winds of racial discrimination and the growing pressure for outright exclusion.

One of the indirect effects of internment was that it marked the end of an era for Japanese bathhouses in the United States. New housing increasingly contained good bathing facilities and Nihonmachi never again were reestablished with the population density and vitality they enjoyed during the prewar years. So too, all things culturally Japanese remained suspect after the bombing of Pearl Harbor. In the wake of internment, many Nisei turned away from their heritage and instead embraced the American dimension of their hybrid identities, making ofuro, shamisen, and other things associated with their parents' generation unattractive.

While Japanese bathhouses never reopened in many western cities after resettlement, Hashidate-Yu enjoyed a brief revival in the postwar years, until operators Fukuo and Shigeko Sano retired in the mid-1960s.

At the time Hashidate-Yu closed it was the last sento or public Japanese bathhouse operating in Seattle and possibly one of the last public bathhouses in the western United States.

Today the Panama Hotel is owned by Jan Johnson, who bought the hotel in 1985 from the Hori family, who had operated it since the 1930s. Jan still runs the Panama as a single-room occupancy residential hotel, maintaining it as a decent and affordable place to live, while retaining its historic character. When the Horis were preparing to sell the building to Jan, they cleaned up the basement and removed most of the trunks that had been stored there since World War II internment, but Jan insisted on keeping as many as possible. These haunting trunks have been included in temporary exhibitions at the Japanese American National Museum and on Ellis Island, but have since been returned to their longstanding home. Along with the bathhouse, these trunks have been featured in the informal tours of the Panama's basement that Jan has led for more than a decade.

Schoolchildren touring the Panama's basement are typically stunned by the sense of entering a completely different time and place. They are intrigued by the communal bathing practices and moved by the vivid lesson in American history evoked by the space and particularly by these dozens of trunks — still unclaimed — that were stored by Japanese Americans on the eve of wartime internment.

In the spring of 1997, Jan began converting a storefront in the building directly above the basement into two bare-bones rooms of brick and wood. It opened as a teahouse in the fall of 2001, decorated with historical photographs of old Japantown and some artifacts from the hotel's basement. The teahouse has begun to restore the sense of Sixth and South Main as the historic center of Seattle's Nihonmachi.

Although the Panama Hotel still stands and its current owner is

Possessions stored on the eve of internment remain in the basement of the Panama Hotel

sensitive to its cultural and historic significance, the fact that sento are no longer in operation evokes a sense of loss among those who once visited them. Mas Fukuhara wishes ofuro were still in operation:

Hashidate-Yu is still a topic of nostalgic conversation among Nisei men. Some of us would still patronize the furo after a round of golf or yard work — or simply to ease the aches and pains of our seventy-year-old-plus carcasses. We wonder why Hashidate Yu was considered a public health hazard by the City of Seattle. Public baths flourish in Japan with no evidence of jeopardy to public health. Over many years of operation we never heard of anyone contracting communicable diseases from patronizing Japan Town's public baths. On the other hand there are many who will testify to the positive physical and psychological benefits from visits to the furo.[19]

The current generation of Japanese Americans did not grow up bathing in sento and typically lack knowledge of the traditional cultural practices associated with it. They are more likely to encounter ofuro on a trip to Japan than in the U.S., as Akemi Kikumura suggests:

Uncle kept urging me to take a bath. I wanted to wash my hair so I asked permission to do so in the bath. Auntie followed me [and] she kindly said, 'I will teach you the Japanese way. We wash ourselves outside the tub before getting in. We get the towel like this [she held the ends and slid it back and forth across her back] and wash. Never put the towel in the clean water. Using this pan, you scoop out the water and wash with it — wash your buttocks and everything. See? So the water is clean because you never scrub in the tub. You are clean before you get in. The bath is just for soaking....it's only the three of us so it's clean. Then at the end of the day, we drain it.' We both laughed. How stupid of me. Yesterday Uncle went to take a bath, got undressed, and found the bath water all gone. I had drained it after getting out.[20]

Preservation of Hashidate-Yu provides Americans of Japanese descent with a tangible reminder of an important aspect of their cultural heritage, and gives all Americans a better understanding of the Japanese imprint on the western landscape.

Chapter 6 **KOKUGO GAKKO** 1414 South Weller Street / **Seattle** / Washington

Principal Yoriaki Nakagawa

Yoriaki Nakagawa's *Common Sense of Japanese and American Etiquette*, published in 1937, advised Issei on the proper display of the American flag; how to navigate the intricacies of Western table settings; and the need for listening closely to English-speakers to avoid creating a bad impression by asking them to repeat themselves.[1] Meanwhile, Principal Nakagawa reminded Nisei children to show their parents proper respect by bowing to them before leaving for school and advised them, among hundreds of other suggestions about decorum, not to loiter on the streets after school let out. Questions surrounding the Americanization of the Issei and the Nisei's tenuous grasp of Japanese cultural norms also stood at the center of Nakagawa's professional concerns as the principal of Seattle's Japanese language school in its heyday before World War II. Seemingly inextricable issues of communication and proper behavior were Nakagawa's focus, whether inscribed in the pages of his etiquette book or enacted in the classrooms of Kokugo Gakko.[2]

Principal Nakagawa's observation that the children tended to loiter on the streets after being released from public school was informed by his unique vantage point atop the steep grade children climbed on the way up Weller Street into Kokugo Gakko each afternoon. From that perch he trained a stern eye on tardy students, knowing that adolescent rebellion among Nisei often took the form of fashionably late arrival at the language school or other undisciplined behavior in the classroom.

But viewed from a Nisei perspective, the daily walk from public school to Kokugo Gakko stood out as a free and easy interlude in what were otherwise long, long days of schooling. As Bill Hosokawa explained:

Until 3 pm the Nisei youngster was exposed to an educational system calculated to make him as good an American as his classmates named O'Brien, Swanson, Santucci or Koblykovich. But when the bell rang and they ran off to play ball, many a Nisei trudged off for another hour or two of classes. Understandably, many Nisei resented the time they had to devote to Japanese language school as well as the discipline they had to endure.[3]

While Nisei attended Kokugo Gakko to learn Japanese, some of their parents braved evening classes in Seattle Public Schools.

If schoolchildren "loitered" at a mom-and-pop grocery along the way — enjoying candy, a soda, or a popsicle — or if they lingered too long on the path between their American and Japanese schools, who could blame them? After all, it was their only break before yet another round of lessons.

Most Issei were quite serious about ensuring their American-born children's Japanese education. Beginning in primary school, those Nisei who attended language school generally went every weekday and six days a week in summer, for eight or more years. In some cases a strong assimilationist ethos led parents to keep their children out of language school; other families were so strapped financially that even the modest cost was prohibitive. Occasionally, older children succeeded in persuading their parents to let them drop out so they could participate in after-school activities. Language school ended prematurely for those Nisei who were still school-age in the winter of 1941-1942, when the principal was arrested along with other Issei leaders and the language school closed for the war's duration.

The intensity of the language school experience goes a long way toward explaining why the reminiscences of former students encompass a wide range of emotions and attitudes — from gratitude for having had the opportunity to learn about their cultural heritage, to resentment over missing out on ordinary childhood pleasures such as participating in after-school sports leagues. While Issei felt pressure to suppress signs of their ethnic identity and demonstrate their capacity to become loyal Americans through assimilation, many of their American-born children chafed under the regimen designed to familiarize them with their Japanese heritage. The buildings that

Images from *Common Sense of Japanese and American Etiquette*

How to Bow to Parents Before Going to School

once housed language schools and which have survived to the present day can be powerful places for exploring intergenerational struggles over competing definitions of identity during the first half of the twentieth century.

Organized in 1902, Seattle's Kokugo Gakko was the first Japanese language school established in the United States. The influx of picture brides and the subsequent birth of the Nisei generation prompted the establishment of language schools wherever Japanese immigrants settled in the United States and its territories, particularly in Hawaii, California, Washington, and Oregon. In California alone more than 250 Japanese language schools were in operation by 1940. Their numbers testify to the growing Nisei population, Issei anxiety over their precarious status in the United States as aliens ineligible for citizenship, and dismay over the manners of their American-born children.[4]

Issei reasoned that if Nisei youth grasped at least the rudiments of Japanese language, history, and culture, the family retained the option of returning home to the mother country if desired or if required by the passage of exclusionary federal immigration policies and restrictive state land laws. Then again, if they ended up settling permanently in the United States, where discrimination sharply limited career opportunities, Issei were comforted by the thought that a basic knowledge of the Japanese language would prepare Nisei youth to work in Issei businesses, even if they could not pursue loftier ambitions.

The language schools played a significant role in shaping the hybrid cultural identity of Nisei by promoting a shared set of cultural norms and, indirectly, by sparking Nisei resistance to

How to Sit During a Reception

How to Present a Gift

being defined by their Japanese ancestry, given that they regarded themselves primarily as Americans. The remaining buildings that once housed Japanese language schools constitute one of the most important historic property types associated with Japanese American heritage in the West. For that reason, and because many are threatened with demolition, greater efforts are now needed to ensure their preservation.

Seattle's Japanese language school began operation in 1902 at the offices of Furuya on Second Avenue. Charitable contributions by visiting Japanese dignitaries seeded formal plans to erect a purpose-built structure within the growing Nihonmachi. The first contribution of $500 was made in 1905 on the occasion of Japanese foreign minister Baron J. Komura's visit to Seattle, at a time when plans for the construction of Nippon Kan Hall already were under way, and there was some thought of incorporating the language school into it.[5] By then, the school had fourteen pupils who were taught Japanese language and literature by Mr. Shibayama, a brother-in-law of C.T. Sasaki, president of the Empire Development Company.[6] Classes were conducted in the rooms of the Japanese Association.[7]

Beginning October 11, 1906, a crisis over Japanese Americans in San Francisco schools prompted other Nikkei communities to debate whether they should remain in public schools; build their own Japanese schools; or supplement public education with after-school training in Japanese language, history, and culture. In June 1908 the *Seattle Times* published the sensational headline: "Japanese to Quit Public Schools: Seattle Orientals Will Educate Their Children Privately."

How to Bow

How to Drink Tea

Seattle Japanese have decided to withdraw their children from the public schools because, [as] alleged at a special meeting of the Japanese Association of the State of Washington, held in the Baker Building last night, the education given is not satisfactory to them. Japanese Schools and Japanese instructors will be substituted for American schools and American instructors, and... [the Nisei] will be instructed in loyalty to the Mikado and the empire of Japan.[8]

   The San Francisco school crisis abated as a result of President Theodore Roosevelt's intervention, and Seattle Issei never actually withdrew their children, who numbered about seventy at the time. By 1910, debate had clearly shifted from favoring the idea of "'pure' Japanese schools," which would have replaced American public schools for Nisei, toward "supplementary education in Japanese ethics, history, geography and language" in an after-school facility.[9] This set the stage for the construction of Kokugo Gakko, Seattle's Japanese language school.

   The movement to construct an independent Japanese language school in Seattle ultimately resulted in the Weller Street facility. According to existing documentation of the historic property, the community raised a little over $10,000 to finance the construction. Issei donated what they could afford, and Japanese nobles, officials, military leaders, and businessmen passing through Seattle, including Baron Kuroki, Baron Komura, and Admiral Yamamoto, contributed according to their status.[10] It was a matter of considerable debate whether their gifts were intended for the school or to benefit the Nikkei community in general.

How to Shut / Open a Door

Greeting an Elder

Kokugo Gakko, 1935

The choice of a western style for the language school building is notable, since wooden clapboard siding and a flat roof stood in sharp contrast to contemporaneous structures such as the Japanese Pavilion at the Alaska-Yukon-Pacific Exposition and the Seattle Buddhist Temple; their designs drew on Japanese architectural conventions, in the first instance authentically and in the second case superficially. After eight years under the auspices of Masajiro Furuya, one of the most prominent Japanese businessmen in the Pacific Northwest, the school moved to a temporary home in the basement of the Seattle Buddhist Temple on South Main Street. There, the school was incorporated by Tatsuya Arai, manager of the Oriental-American Bank, and C. Tetsuo Takahashi, president of both the Oriental-American Bank and the Oriental Trading Company. In 1913, the same year that the Japanese Teachers Association of America was founded, Seattle's Issei and Nisei celebrated the opening of a new school building on Weller Street, designed by Japanese immigrant architect S. Shimizu. The first class in the new building included ninety-eight students. By 1917 attendance had grown to the point that a second building was added. A third building, known as the portable, erected early in the 1920s, completed the language school facilities.

**Japanese Pavilion at the
Alaska-Yukon-Pacific Exposition**

The growing need for this final building coincided with vigorous public debate over exclusion, as the Congressional Committee on Immigration held hearings in the Seattle area about whether Japanese were capable of assimilation and the Washington State legislature finally passed its own Alien Land Laws. In the face of rising hostility in the 1920s, language schools tended to "reframe their mission to include Americanization," either as a strategic response to the unfavorable publicity they were receiving from exclusionists or as a result of hostile state legislation that regulated the selection of teachers, use of educational materials, or other practices at foreign language schools.[11] The decade before World War II witnessed a peak in the population of school-aged Nisei, many of whom attended language school. During the 1930s, approximately 1,800 children attended Seattle's Japanese Language School on a daily basis. As a result, the language school came to occupy a critical place in the collective memory of the Nisei generation.

Now-elderly Nisei who attended Seattle's Japanese language school in the prewar period used several names for the school, although they can no longer recall what some of them meant. Their memory encompassed the transition from Nihongo Gakko to Kokugo Gakko, which reflected the immigrant community's effort to shift public perception from a school to an institute.

Seattle Buddhist Temple

This name change was intended to mollify critics by signaling the school's subordination to public school education. More cryptically, a number of former students referred to it as Typ School, a nick-name whose precise meaning has been lost over the years, though one woman was sure it meant that "we all thought it was a jerk school," which left her friends laughing hard. This echoes Bill Hosokawa's interpretation, which draws on a 1934 article by Aiji Tashiro published in *New Outlook* magazine:

There was a class of Japanese that I called Typs. This was an abbreviation for typical Jap. A Typ usually needed a haircut or had too obviously just had one…His father ran a grocery store, his sisters finished high school and worked in a market. The Typ was enviably proficient in math and in art; totally lacking in the finer points of social grace. His clothes were incongruous and misfit. He either slunk timidly in the society of Americans or assumed a defiant, truculent air. He was impervious to self-consciousness, if the latter class, and persisted in jabbering loudly in Japanese in the presence of Americans. All Typs cliqued together in school and out. The timid kind went on to college and became Phi Beta Kappas and Doctors. The brazen variety became the denizens of pool halls and street corners. I decided that I was not a Typ.

Hosokawa notes that "the Japanese language school in Seattle where Tashiro grew up was widely referred to as Typ School."[12]

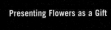
Presenting Flowers as a Gift

How to Sit

Reminiscences of language school alumni suggest that the building and the activities it housed simply did not have the same meaning for the Nisei students who attended it as it did for Issei founders. The first generation saw it, at least partially, as an insurance policy that at minimum guaranteed their ability to communicate with their American-born children and at maximum provided them with an escape clause should things get so bad in the U. S. that they decided to return permanently to Japan. In contrast, the Nisei mostly saw language school as an imposition on their freedom.

Although there were some very disciplined students, by and large those who attended the language school, boys in particular, resented its imposition on their playtime and would have preferred to participate in organized sports. If it was difficult to fully interest American-born children of Japanese descent in learning the Japanese language, efforts to train them in the intricacies of Japanese etiquette, while perhaps met with superficial compliance, marked the real distance between Issei and Nisei expectations. Remembering occasional visits paid to the school by dignitaries, one former student prodded her peers,

Do you remember when they used to have dignitaries come to call at Kokugo Gakko? They used our gym and we all had to file in and we stood there and they told us to bow and we would bow and then nobody would listen to what ever it was and then we would all have to march back to school? [13]

食器の並べ方 (一)

Dining

Visitors to the Kokugo Gakko, 1927.

The sternness and solemnity of Issei men was alienating to their American-born children, whose critical perspective on adult behavior seemed to be increased from the vantage point of the long walk up the steps of the language school, past the principal's office, or from the audience of Nippon Kan Hall on ceremonial occasions.

As the students reached high school age, it was increasingly difficult for the teachers — often the mothers of Kokugo Gakko students — to control the behavior of some of the boys who, according to Tama Tokuda, "just went wild." One man recalled,

They tried to be strict but I remember the teachers, I mean the students just about ran the teachers ragged. I mean some of them [were] really mean. And it got to the point I think the teachers dreaded it about as much as the kids did. But we did learn.[14]

Sam Shoji was one student at Kokugo Gakko who avowedly spent a substantial portion of his language school education "in the principal's office," for pulling pranks and distracting the class. Sam explained that,

At that time, the teachers were interested in teaching us the language, but also a lot of the culture: discipline, history and typical things taught in school in Japan. Well, speaking for myself, I wasn't too interested in it. I was tired and I wanted to play, so the Japanese Language School became my playground, both in and out of the classrooms.[15]

Before class ended, Sam added coal to the classroom stove, knowing his teacher couldn't leave until it burned out. Even Principal Nakagawa, who ran the school "with an iron fist," occasionally met his match in sheer willfulness, as Kokugo Gakko teacher Tamaki Nagai recounted:

Since all of the students in my classes worked so hard to learn Japanese, nothing extraordinary happened; but in other classes there were some students who were beyond the teachers' control. For example, after school one of the women teachers asked Principal Nakagawa to discipline a certain student. I was there at the time and heard the student. When he was scolded, he called the Principal, 'ojisan' (old man). I reproached him, saying, 'The Principal is not ojisan! Call him sensei! (teacher)." But the student repeatedly said 'ojisan, ojisan.' In the end Mr. Nakagawa sighed and said with a grin on his face, 'Boy, he's audacious!'[16]

Milder forms of resistance were the by-product of accumulated resentment fused with adolescent rebellion on the part of fundamentally good kids.

I was quite devoted to the Japanese language school for many years… I can't remember when I quit but maybe I was going to high school or something. And I noticed that all the other students who had, aside from the Asian ones, you know, enjoyed school activities so much. And then I started to resent going to Japanese School. And in fact, I think it was when you were about 13, 14, 15 it was considered fashionable to go there late.[17]

Yet the fact that Japanese Americans lived in a tightly knit community meant that parents would soon learn about the most minor transgressions. As one Kokugo Gakko alum noted, "no wonder the teacher used to come over crying to our house. We lived across the street [so] it was easy for them to traipse across."[18]

For Nisei who attended the Japanese language school, the most memorable places seemed to lie outside the formal architecture of home

"I was amazed to learn that Nakagawa-san wrote a book on etiquette. Well, after having written such a book, he was focused on us like a laser beam in regard to our deportment. Now his intensity in molding us makes sense. We were such ungrateful subjects."

Monica Sone
January 11, 2001

NISEI DAUGHTER

Monica Sone's autobiographical novel, *Nisei Daughter*, suggests that Issei-controlled spaces such as Kokugo Gakko carried many expectations about traditional behavior. Above, Monica Sone with her mother.

Gradually I yielded to my double dose of schooling. Nihon Gakko was so different from grammar school I found myself switching my personality back and forth daily like a chameleon. At Bailey Gazert School I was a jumping, screaming, roustabout Yankee, but at the stroke of three when the school bell rang and doors burst open everywhere, spewing pupils like jelly beans from a broken bag, I suddenly became a modest, faltering, earnest little Japanese girl with a small, timid voice. I trudged down a steep hill and climbed up another steep hill to Nihon Gakko with other black-haired girls and boys. On the playground, we behaved cautiously. Whenever we spied a teacher within bowing distance, we hissed at each other to stop the game, put our feet neatly together, slid our hands down to our knees and bowed slowly and sanctimoniously. In just the proper, moderate tone, putting in every ounce of respect, we chanted, "Konichi-wa, sensei. Good day."

For an hour and a half each day, we were put through our paces. At the beginning of each class hour, Yasuda-sensei punched a little bell on her desk. We stood up by our seats, at strict attention. Another "ping!" We all bowed to her in unison while she returned the bow solemnly. With the third "ping!" we sat down together.

There was yomi-kata time when individual students were called upon to read the day's lesson, clear and loud. The first time I recited I stood and read with swelling pride the lesson which I had prepared the night before. I mouthed each word carefully and paused for the proper length of time at the end of each sentence. Suddenly Yasuda-sensei stopped me.

"Kazuko-san!"

I looked up at her confused, wondering what mistakes I had made.

"You are holding your book in one hand," she accused me. Indeed, I was. I did not see the need of using two hands to support a thin book which I could balance with two fingers.

"Use both hands," she commanded me.

Then she peered at me. "And are you leaning against your desk?" Yes, I was, slightly. "Stand up straight!"

"Hai! Yes, ma'am!"

I learned that I could stumble all around in my lessons without ruffling the sensei's nerves, but it was a personal insult to her if I displayed sloppy posture. I must stand up like a soldier, hold the book high in the air with both hands, and keep my feet still.

As time went on, I began to suspect that there was much more to Nihon Gakko than learning the Japanese language. There was a driving spirit of strict discipline behind it all which reached and weighed heavily upon each pupil's consciousness.

Girls doing calisthenics at Kokugo Gakko picnic, 1930's.

and school. Consistently, they waxed poetic about their daily walk between schools, unsupervised by adults. As Shigeki (Paul) Kaseguma recalled:

Our biggest deal was going home — I mean going from [one] school to the other. There was a hamburger place. One man just sold it and he would have a greasy hamburger with chili spread on it. That was big deal for us.

A brief stop at the local candy store was memorable as well.

There was a Japanese store, a mom and pop store, [where] we looked forward to spending our pennies at the candy counter. For 2 cents or something, you could get this mint — the inside was white. But occasionally [in] this whole mass of a container, there were one or two that had a pink inside. And if you got a pink inside, you could get something free. So all of us, you know we gambled on that candy. I don't think I ever got it. [19]

For a precious few minutes each day, Japanese American children existed outside the discipline of home and school. Thus, the streets hold a special place in their memory, as do the close friendships forged in those years.

Likewise, annual spring picnics held in local parks were remembered fondly because they were exclusively devoted to innocent amusements. Mothers would make bento and share, with the customary disclaimer, "This isn't much or this doesn't taste good, but here, have some of ours." While these gatherings were clearly benign occasions, anti-Japanese sentiment ran so high that some whites panicked at the sight of Japanese gathering in one place, as a March 1908 article in the *Seattle Times* documents:

That there are more Japanese in Seattle and vicinity than is apparent to most people was forcibly illustrated to the citizens of South Park last Sunday, when 2,000 subjects of the Mikado assembled on the Cavanaugh tract in the suburb and held a picnic. A few of the suburban residents are still of the opinion that the Japanese have had some motive in holding the meeting other than mere innocent amusement, but leading Japanese of the city say that the only object of their countrymen was to have a good time, as is the custom in Japan in the spring of each year. [20]

Surely the most troubling sign was the incorporation of the Japanese flag into calisthenic exercises. In response, many immigrants felt compelled to hide signs of cultural difference whenever they were being watched. Banzo Okada of Seattle remembered:

In the storm of exclusion, many Japanese went on picnics over the holidays, but when they saw the shadow of a white man they quietly hid their native foods and their chopsticks. Thinking back on all these things, I realize that there is nothing peculiar in eating these things now, but since we were usually stoned and despised as 'Japs,' whenever we saw a sign of the whites we were instinctively on guard. [21]

Fortunately the children's attention usually was focused on the gunnysack and spoon races, ice cream bars, and strawberry soda pop. On these rare occasions, parents and teachers stepped out of their usual role as disciplinarians and joined in the games, much to the children's delight: "Usually they are so solemn, you know, but here they tried to win the race and they looked real funny to us!" The day usually ended in a mock battle among the boys. As Sam Shoji recalled,

You took a sugar cone, put a string through it and tied it on your head. Then you got a newspaper stick and used that to try to swat the cones off

Women in footrace at Kokugo Gakko picnic, 1918.

"Usually the Language School teachers were so solemn, but here at the picnic they tried to win the race…they looked real funny to us!"

SAM SHOJI

FORMER STUDENT AT KOKUGO GAKKO

A classroom in the portable building, 1997.

of people's heads. Sometimes you got the head, but the one who had the cone left at the end was the winner. Boy did the ice cream fly! [22]

Ironically, this brief inversion of the usual decorum served to reinforce normal behavioral expectations during the other days of the year.

One of the lasting consequences of the internment of people of Japanese descent from the West Coast during World War II was the end of language schools. The principals and teachers were targeted for early arrest as visible community leaders who were associated with an institution suspected of fostering allegiances with enemy Japan. Schools were closed and the residents of the West Coast communities in which language schools were located were imprisoned during the war. In the process, latent hostility and overt propaganda tainted all things Japanese as disloyal to America. Those who resettled in West Coast cities in the postwar period frequently did not return to Nihonmachi; like many Americans, those of Japanese descent frequently settled in the suburbs. Finally, it would be the Nisei, not the Issei, who had to make decisions about how to shape the ethnic identities of their children after 1945. The fact that their perceived "otherness" had led them to be interned, despite their status as American citizens, combined with their own history of resentment over having had to attend language schools as children, undermined the position of such schools in the postwar period.

In a few cases, Seattle's Japanese language school prominent among them, community groups have reclaimed their language schools as key social and cultural institutions. They have had to adapt to changing conditions, however, since the language schools no longer serve as vehicles for socializing a whole generation, as Kokugo Gakko did from 1902 to 1941. After serving as temporary housing for those resettling from the camps,[23] Seattle's Japanese American community reclaimed the facilities

for use as a language school in 1956. The Northwest Nikkei Museum opened in two rooms of the Seattle Language School in October of 1998, providing a lasting place to display historic documents and artifacts related to Japanese Americans in the Pacific Northwest. Language school classes are now taught on Saturday mornings. They serve families dedicated to providing their children with a stronger sense of their heritage. In recognition of the language school's historical significance, the property was listed on the National Register of Historic Places in 1982. Part of the effort to manage the large facility has included the application of vinyl siding, but otherwise little has changed.

The buildings still possess many of the interior details needed to send former students into an ambivalent reverie upon seeing the dark wooden planks at the entry and hearing their familiar creak near the principal's office, "just like it used to do in those days." The old blackboards that remain in each classroom evoke the memory of toban duties that students were required to perform: cleaning the blackboard and clapping the erasers to remove accumulated chalk dust. Gazing at the main building from a distance, one still senses Principal Nakagawa's formidable presence, dressed in a black suit, standing at his usual post by the front door. First he looks down at his watch, then up the block. Listening closely, it's almost possible to hear the children's laughter until he catches their eyes, gestures for them to come in, and admonishes them — "Isoite Irasshai!" — to hurry along to classes that have already begun.

Because the vast majority of Japanese immigrants practiced Buddhism, Buddhist temples and churches were among the most significant buildings established in American Nihonmachi. Historically, Japanese Buddhism has not operated as a single unified religion, and immigrants to the United States represent five subdivisions of Buddhism, of which most have practiced Jodo Shinshu or True Pure Land Buddhism.[1]

On July 30, 1898, an inaugural ceremony for the Young Men's Buddhist Association (YMBA) of San Francisco was held, including the adoption of a constitution and the election of a board of directors, thereby creating the first Jodo Shinshu organization in America.[2] By 1910 the number of Buddhist churches and temples in the U.S. had increased to twenty, and they were distributed along the West Coast, stretching from Los Angeles to Seattle.[3]

Buddhist churches soon assumed an expanded and unifying role within their communities. The influx of Japanese women to the U.S. during the picture-bride era (1908-21) fostered the development of stable family life in the Japanese immigrant community and shifted the role of Buddhist churches away from serving a predominantly male sangha (congregation) toward meeting the needs of young families.[4] Fujinkai (women's auxiliaries) were established and began to engage in activities that involved food preparation for church-related functions. Large kitchens began to

Left to right:
Visalia Buddhist Church and
detail, 1941; Stockton
Buddhist Church, constructed
1969; Idaho-Oregon
Buddhist Temple and detail,
constructed 1958.

be incorporated into churches to house equipment for the preparation of massive quantities of rice, tea, and other culturally significant foods.[5] Most American Protestants viewed Buddhism as a strange religion, and early Buddhist sangha often chose to blend their temples into the surrounding neighborhood by using rented space; converting existing houses; or constructing simple, wood-framed buildings as places to gather.

Prior to World War II, the church continued to grow in importance within Nikkei communities. From 1920 to 1941, twenty-one new Buddhist churches were established in the U.S., at a time when exclusionary immigration policies and anti-Japanese agitation brought suspicion to all things Japanese.[6] Unwelcome within the mainstream of American culture, Japanese Americans turned to ethnic associations for links to their heritage and created social, economic, and political organizations centered on Buddhist churches. Secular programs, including picnics, language schools, and rotating credit systems, were combined with religious activities. As the church became more family-focused in this period, Sunday schools, church gatherings, "American-style" dances, and athletic events for youth became important social functions.[7] To accommodate growing sangha, ancillary church buildings were constructed including gymnasiums, meeting halls, Japanese language schools, dorms, and ministers' residences.[8] Church architecture assumed a more monumental

form in this period. Some churches drew upon popular Western architectural styles; others incorporated Japanese design elements, replicating specific periods of Japanese temple architecture. In these cases, the availability of Japanese carpenters allowed communities to build places of worship in the traditional manner, without nails, using post-and-beam construction and notched wood joints. The Enmanji Buddhist Temple, which still stands in Sebastopol, California, is an outstanding example of a twelfth century Kamakura-style Japanese temple, with an unusual history.[9]

"Three carpenters from San Francisco built the church. When construction started, these three men went up, and one man threw little rice cakes to everybody."

Yoneko "Pat" Shimizu, daughter of Tomotaro Kobuke, Enmanji temple founder

On April 15, 1934, an Ochigo procession wound from downtown Sebastopol to the outskirts of town to mark the opening of Sonoma County's Enmanji Temple, a branch of the San Francisco based Buddhist Churches of America (BCA). Hundreds of Japanese American families, whether Buddhist or not, gathered for the procession, which featured a parade band and children dressed in elaborate traditional clothing. The celebration was timed to coincide with Hanamatsuri, the date marking the Buddha's birthday.[10] A traditional arch of evergreen boughs was positioned near the new temple building. Originally designed for the Japanese exhibit at the 1933 Century of Progress Exposition in Chicago, the temple — made by Japanese carpenters of hand-carved wood — had served as an exhibit hall for the South Manchurian Railway Company. Constructed in Japan and shipped in pieces to Chicago, the temple was rebuilt by Japanese carpenters as a faithful replica of a Kamakura Period structure.[11]

World's Fairs had been an important venue for introducing Japanese arts and architecture to the United States. The first large display of Japanese design at the 1876 Centennial Exhibition in Philadelphia created many admirers of Japanese aesthetics, including some American architects who developed an interest in Japanese design and construction methods.[12] The Japanese government created exhibits for several of the World's Fairs in the decades that followed, including the influential World's Columbian Exposition of 1893 that was held in Chicago. The simplicity and structural honesty of Chicago's Phoenix Villa presented a stark contrast to the imposing neoclassical structures that inspired the fair's nickname — the "White City." Patterned after an eleventh-century temple near Kyoto, Phoenix Villa's complex of unpainted plaster and timbered framework lived on after the fair as a museum and tea garden for nearly fifty years.[13]

HUNDREDS SEE NEW JAPANESE TEMPLE OPENED

Buddhist Temple at Sebastopol Dedicated With Ancient Rites

With hundreds of Japanese from all parts of Northern California participating, Emanji Temple, at Sebastopol, the only Buddhist temple in the United States, was dedicated Sunday with elaborate Buddhistic rites.

Ceremonies were started at 10 o'clock Sunday morning with the Rev. Akahoshi and the Rev. Tsukamoto in charge. They were assisted by Naoki Wakaye, Chigogi Sakaguchi and M. Otani and other officials of the church, in the colorful ritualistic work.

Buddhist rites dating back many centuries were performed for the first time in the United States during the dedication.

Among them was the march of the "chigo," with more than 150 school children from all parts of Northern California participating. Dressed in colorful ceremonial robes of Ancient pattern, and wearing elaborate gold headdresses, the children, accompanied by high Buddhist dignitaries, a band, and a group of young men in white robes, bearing on their shoulders a flower-decked shrine, marched from Nippon hall, in Sebastopol, to the temple, a mile from the city.

Carrying white and pink lotus flowers, beautiful symbols of the Buddhist faith, the tiny marchers walked slowly into the temple grounds and around the building while the temple bell was tolled by one of the officiating priests.

Following the march of the "chigo," temple priests conducted solemn services in the temple, chanting the words of the service from their stand in front of the gold-decked shrine that occupies one entire end of the building.

BUDDHIST TEMPLE DEDICATED AT SEBASTOPOL

園満寺
新築落成
遷佛慶讃 大法要御案内

一九三三年の夏米國シカゴに開催された世界博覧會へ満洲帝國と南満洲鐵道會社より出品さ
れを桑港佛敎會支部ソノマ佛敎會へ再下附せらるゝこと〲なりましたので一九三三年十一
月十七日シアトルを經てソノマ郡セバストポールに移送しました。

之れに先立ち同年一月十六日親慈聖人御忌会
たしました。

爾來若江技師棟梁となり、坂口技師信徒
慶賀に堪へません。

時恰も釋尊降誕二千五百年の春を迎へ永
無二の法城完成を見たることは實に喜びの
鎌倉時代の古典的優雅なる満洲館は北米
を擧げるべく今後幾百萬の人類救濟の根本
世は不景氣のドン底にあり乍らかゝる
の加庇力に依ることは勿論、信徒各位の
謝いたします。

兹に落成の祝意を表はさんがため來る
ます故何卒同日同刻迄に御家内打ち揃つ

ENMANJI BUDDHIST TEMPLE   Sebastopol / California [131]

"My dad used to send us to the Baptist Church. Every Sunday, we'd get up and he'd give us a nickel, and we'd take [it] to the church for offering. He wanted us to have religious instruction. That's why he said, 'We have to have a Buddhist Church here for the young people."

YONEKO SHIMIZU
ENMANJI TEMPLE MEMBER

Enmanji Buddhist Temple, 1934.
The building was formerly part of the Japanese exhibit at
the 1933 Century of Progress Exposition in Chicago.

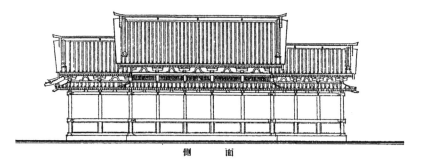

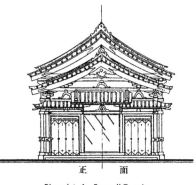

正　　面

Blueprints for Enmanji Temple

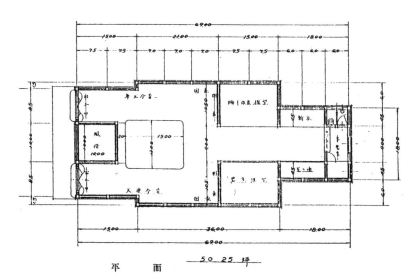

側　　面

平　　面　　　　50.25 坪

Although Enmanji Temple and Phoenix Villa share beginnings in Chicago World's Fairs, their histories provide a revealing contrast. The villa modified a sacred building form to secular uses, which were offered as a means to amuse and educate Americans about Japanese culture. The Enmanji building, also inspired by a historic temple, was used for similar purposes in its brief incarnation as the South Manchurian Railway Exhibit. Its unlikely journey to Sonoma County brought the structure full circle as it assumed the role of spiritual and social center for a Japanese American community.

Enmanji Buddhist Temple grew from the desire of Issei generation parents for a place to pass on traditions of culture and worship they had brought from Japan. Members of the community had established a Buddhist Sunday School and an affiliated Japanese language school in 1926.[14] The temple began as a small fellowship and branch of the San Francisco Buddhist Church and declared its autonomy as the Sonoma County Buddhist Church in April 1932. The U.S. Census of two years earlier had recorded 716 foreign-born Japanese in Sonoma County, most of whom lived in or near the town of Sebastopol. Residents of an agricultural landscape filled with small towns, fruit orchards, and chicken farms, most Japanese Americans in the area worked on the land in some capacity. Some owned apple orchards or apple dehydrating plants. Others grew prunes, hops, and grapes or raised the chickens on which the area prided itself.[15]

Putting down roots in this area of Northern California meant establishing a place where the major turning points in individual lives and in the community's development could be marked, remembered, and celebrated. On November 5, 1933, the members of the church met to discuss a proposal for a free building from their parent organization, the Buddhist Mission of North America. Bishop Kenyo Masuyama had negotiated the gift of the South Manchurian Railway building and was, in turn, offering it to the Sonoma group. Despite the difficulties presented by the Depression economy, a successful house-to-house fundraising drive secured the money necessary to move the disassembled building by rail and reconstruct it in Sebastopol.[16]

Yoneko "Pat" Shimizu, whose father was one of the temple founders, remembered that "there were three carpenters from San Francisco who built the church. When construction started, these three men went up and one man threw little rice cakes to everybody," as part of the traditional Muneage ceremony.[17] Early services were held in Japanese, which served as a barrier to younger people who had not attended (or who had not been diligent students at) Japanese language

1933 World's Fair poster for the Manchuria Exhibit

school.[18] Yet the temple offered a wide array of activities — from community wide holiday celebrations to the women's Fujinkai service group to the sports and social events of the Young Buddhists Association.

Temple membership came from Sonoma and the adjacent counties of Mendocino, Marin, and Napa. Many temple-sponsored events, however, welcomed the Japanese American community as a whole. The spring Hanamatsuri Festival of Flowers and summer Obon Odori dance commemorating ancestors were (and continue to be) popular community wide events. Enmanji-sponsored picnics in county parks brought Buddhists and non-Buddhists together, as did performances of traditional noh plays staged at the temple.[19]

These activities, along with the community life they fostered, were brought to a halt by the evacuation of Sonoma County Japanese Americans to Amache Relocation Center in Granada, Colorado. Unlike many evacuees from other parts of the state, who faced intense anti-Japanese sentiment, most were able to enlist friends and neighbors to care for their homes and possessions while they were interned. The temple itself was closed and, despite the guardianship of those nearby, the building suffered several

acts of vandalism during those years. Evidence of the attacks is preserved in one charred area of the temple ceiling; upon their return from internment, the temple board voted to keep this section of the ceiling as a reminder of that painful time.[20]

Enmanji Buddhist Temple was reopened and repaired in the years after the war, and a new wave of community building grew around the temple. By the early 1950s, the facility was straining to accommodate the myriad church and social activities held there. In 1953, construction began on Memorial Hall, with space for Sunday school classes as well as for social and recreational events for the larger community. Built by community volunteers, Memorial Hall was dedicated in 1954 to the memory of three local Nisei men who lost their lives serving in the all-Nisei 442nd Regimental Combat Team, among the most highly decorated units in World War II.[21]

In contrast to the traditional form of the Enmanji Buddhist Temple, new Buddhist churches constructed after World War II frequently embraced popular modern architectural styles of the 1950s and 1960s, yet still incorporated some elements of Japanese style and symbolism in a very

Sacramento Obon festival, 2001

First Seattle Bon Odori, 1932

O B O N AND B O N   O D O R I

Obon is a Buddhist event and an important Japanese tradition. According to Japanese belief, the souls of one's ancestors return to their homes during Obon. Altars are set up in the home to welcome the ancestors' souls. Offerings of vegetables, rice dumplings, noodles, and fruits may be made. Families light chochin (lanterns) in front of their houses to guide the spirits of the dead safely on the journey from their graves to the family home.

During Obon, bon odori (folk dances) are held all over Japan. The specific type of dance varies from area to area. A temporary platform (yagura) is set up in an open space. Lanterns are tied to the yagura. A drummer inside the yagura supplies the beat for the dance. The dancers in their kimono and yukata circle the yagura.

Enmanji Temple Teriyaki Barbecue, July 1954.

restrained manner.[22] Meanwhile, the popular American conception of Buddhism as an aesthetically stark and rigorous spiritual practice was shaped by Zen Buddhism, which was brought to the West by Japanese teachers after World War II and adopted primarily by non-Asians. Zendo (meditation halls) in this tradition are designed without seats, other than pillows used for zazen (sitting meditation) in an open, spare hall with a simple altar. In contrast, non-Buddhists entering most Jodo Shinshu temples, or, for that matter, temples of other Buddhist sects with a Japanese American sangha, may be surprised to find them organized in a fashion similar to Christian churches. Pews or chairs are arranged in a nave, and a pulpit and an organ or piano stand in front near the image of the Buddha.[23]

Today, the Enmanji Temple Teriyaki Barbecue, first established in the postwar period, remains a popular public event and a successful fund-raiser. Each year, temple members pour their energies and skills into this major event, which serves thousands of meals built around that local favorite, the Petaluma chicken. Over time, a crafts bazaar and Japanese cultural displays and demonstrations were added to the affair, which inspired similar chicken teriyaki events at Buddhist churches throughout California.[24]

Tucked under generous awnings behind Memorial Hall are the cinder blocks used to construct huge barbecue pits needed to host the teriyaki event, along with dozens of giant rice steamers and a plethora of cooking utensils and appliances. The informal chaos of the scene lies steps away from the imposing temple structure and a new Japanese garden lovingly planted on Enmanji grounds by a local nursery owner and his family. The entire constellation is a remarkable testament to the strength of a community and its ability to create a place that joins its traditions with the present.

岡山縣苫田郡鏡野村大字竹田

下市北町十一ノ一
北町十一ノ六五

長女　千代子　明治四十一年五月十九日生
次男　孝　一　同十二年六月二十日生
四男　輝　男　大正五年十二月二十三日生
五男　瀧次郎

三男　貞　男
大正三年一月二十一日生

牧野

Chapter 8

KUWABARA HOSPITAL + MIDWIFERY

565 and 580 North Fifth Street / **San Jose** / California

Japanese American communities expanded rapidly during the first two decades of the twentieth century as women and children joined the male workers who had shaped the first wave of immigration. As families formed and grew, health care and medical facilities became a pressing concern. Skilled practitioners were needed to deal with the increasing number of childbirths. Midwives were well-respected figures in Japanese American communities. The birth stories of most Nisei involved one of only a few sanba (midwives) who served each community.

Japanese hospitals and midwiferies were critical community institutions in urban Nihonmachi such as Los Angeles's Little Tokyo and Seattle's Japantown, as well as in the agricultural centers of Sacramento and San Jose. San Jose's Kuwabara Hospital, built by the Nishiura Brothers in 1910, served this purpose. This chapter honors the Kuwabara Hospital, one of the earliest Japanese medical centers on the West Coast, and the more modest building that housed the midwifery of Mito Hori across the street. Understanding the significance of these historic properties, however, requires a detour into the experience of Issei women who lacked access to such a facility.

Issei women who worked with their husbands on farms in more remote locations, on Vashon or Bainbridge Island in Washington's Puget Sound, or in settlements associated with extraction industries such as logging or fishing, rarely were able to get a midwife to their house in time to attend the birth of their children. In such cases, women sometimes gave birth on their own or turned to their husband for assistance. As Yoshiko Ueda of Spokane explained:

First we lived in a tent-house, and during the winter it was so cold one couldn't sleep. Therefore we made a bed in the barn out of scrap lumber, spread straw on the frame, and on top of that put the [comforters] which we had brought from Japan. I delivered my daughter in this stable, and since there was no doctor or nurse, my husband was the midwife.[1]

Gin Okazaki of Vashon Island presented a similar picture of the birth of her first child, from the vantage point of rural Vashon Island:

Then my baby was due to be born. If we had a midwife we would have to pay from $20 to $50, and doctors were even more expensive. Transportation was bad on Vashon Island, besides, and so we couldn't easily get hold of either a midwife or doctor. As a result, in every family the husband played the role of midwife. My husband had had no experience as a midwife, but he had a friend who had once helped in an emergency and had safely delivered the baby, so my husband went to him to ask how he did it. The important thing is how to cut the umbilical cord. First you tie it tightly with string in two places. Then cut in between the tied places with a pair of scissors. When the time came, my husband and I, one way or another, cut the cord and delivered a beautiful baby. [2]

Those who lived in remote areas found it difficult to get a midwife's help in the relatively short time between the onset of contractions and childbirth. As a result, some of the more experienced mothers began to serve others in rural communities. Chiyo Hisayasu of Spokane explained that

The most difficult thing for a farm woman was the delivery of a baby. I was blessed with five boys and five girls in South Park, and until just before delivery I always worked, big stomach and all. When I finally gave birth, it was always a man who served as midwife. I got used to it. But as I had heard that the umbilical cord is most important, I cut it and took care of it myself. Since I delivered ten babies, I became an expert and frequently went to other people as a midwife. [3]

Perhaps the most dramatic cases of isolation were experienced by those who lived on the tidal flats of Washington while working for the oyster industry. Japanese immigrants working for the J. J. Brenner Company lived in what were called stations or float-houses. This unusual form of workers' housing was built several miles out on the tidal flats of Willapa Bay, Oyster Bay, Mud Bay, and an inlet of Skookum Bay.[4]

晩香坡ダンレビー街一四三

山口縣玖珂郡神代村

宇野　亀惑

長男　正秀

大正四年八月十日生

晩香坡市

高知縣高岡郡新井村

中島寅太郎

長女　文

"Takahashi [my husband] wrote back to me in Japan to learn midwifery because Japanese pregnant women who lived in San Francisco didn't understand English and needed a Japanese midwife very badly. That's why I decided to study midwifery before leaving Japan."

KAMECHIYO TAKAHASHI

SAN FRANCISCO MIDWIFE

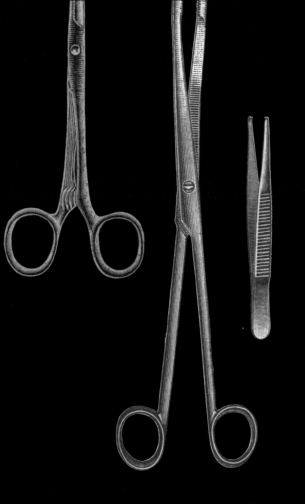

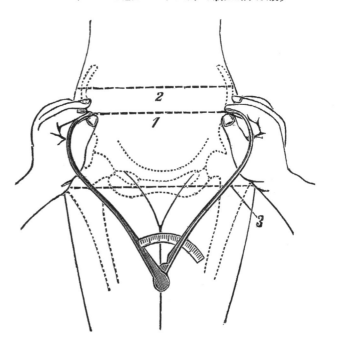

Illustration from a Japanese midwifery textbook.

（腸骨前上棘を計測するに状態を示す）

The station was set on top of a platform supported by 50-foot long pillars driven into the ocean floor. Sometimes the oyster stations or float-houses were occupied by five or six coworkers; other times by families. One measure of the isolation of those who lived and worked out of float-houses was their extremely limited recreational opportunities: an annual picnic and a round of visits by boat at the New Year. They also looked forward to an occasional visit to the "big city," in this case Olympia, to stock up on groceries.[5]

Barely warmed by a wood stove and illuminated by an oil lamp, husband and wife or co-workers sat at the table and sorted the oysters late into the night. During the harvest, the oyster men worked out on the water in the pitch-dark night, where it was easy to lose their way. As Susumu Sato remembered, "The fog sometimes was very dense, and it took us eight hours or so wandering around on the ocean just looking for our home-sweet-home."[6] As Kiyoichi Miyahara noted,

Sometimes I couldn't sleep all night for thinking that the house might drift off, or the sculls and floats tied to the house might carry it away. [7]

Out of season, the men engaged in other activities associated with oystering, including repairing the floats and breaks in the dike and replanting oyster seeds. Besides oysters, those living in the float-houses also caught perch, salmon, octopus, seaweed of various kinds, and clams, all of which were abundant. Getting water, fuel, and fresh vegetables proved difficult for those dwelling out in the tidal flats. Capturing clean rainwater was not always easy, as gulls could easily contaminate the run-off from the roof. As Takeji Minegishi explained,

The station was three miles from land, and so we used the rain water from the roof. A round tank was installed which could contain a considerable supply of water. Since seagulls frequently perched on the roof of the station, it is certain that we drank some of their dirt! [8]

Float-house dwellers bought fresh vegetables on rare trips to Olympia, purchased supplies from representatives of import/export companies such as Furuya, planted a garden in the company's open lot, and, according to Takeji Minegishi, even improvised a "'four-square-yard plantation' on the

Oyster stations were set on platforms supported by fifty-foot pillars driven into the ocean floor.

Japanese American workers sorting oysters.

float."[9] With water all around, the float house was a difficult place to raise a family. Kiyoichi Miyahara described the ocean life as similar to being "raised in a cage."[10]

It could also be deadly dangerous. As Takeji Minegishi explained: "Since we lived in a house built on the sea, occasionally a child would fall overboard and drown. These dead children were buried in the Masonic Cemetery in Olympia."[11]

The remote location of the oyster houses also made it impossible to rely on doctors or midwives attending births, as Kiyoichi Miyahara recalled. "When my wife delivered babies, I asked a neighboring old lady to help her, and went to shore by boat and telephoned the doctor in Olympia. It took three or four hours before the doctor came. By the time he got there, the baby would be delivered."[12] Thus, the conditions of childbirth differed considerably for Issei living in urban areas and on the periphery.

In contrast to those who settled in more remote locations, the Issei who lived in towns and cities with well-developed Nihonmachi, from 1910 on, had ready access to midwives to ease the Nisei's transition into the world. San Jose's Kuwabara Hospital, and the midwifery of Mito Hori across North Fifth Street, served Japanese American clients from throughout Santa Clara County. Financed by the Kumamoto Kenjinkai, Kuwabara Hospital is one of the earliest Japanese American medical centers on the West Coast, and the oldest known example still standing.[13] The Colonial Revival structure was built in 1910 by the Nishiura Brothers, a construction firm that also worked on Japanese Pavilions for the Panama Pacific World's Fair in 1915 and the Treasure Island Exposition of 1933. Gentaro and Shinzaburo Nishiura built a stylistically diverse set of landmarks in San Jose's Japantown, including the Buddhist Church Betsuin only one block north of the hospital.[14]

One of the Nishiura sons recalled that although his father followed the Shinto religion, he had gone into great debt to build the traditionally crafted Buddhist church, which was dedicated in 1937. The third in a series of structures housing the Nihonmachi's Buddhist religious activities, the building is considered one of the most authentic Japanese-style Buddhist temples in the United States. Harry Nishiura recalled that his father's commitment to the building was so great that he rushed to put out a nighttime fire there in 1941 despite a 6 p.m. curfew on Japanese Americans.

"Our house was made from half of an older elementary school building. My dad had his dentist office in the front. We lived in the middle section and my grandmother practiced as a midwife in the back.

My grandmother kept her patients in the house for five days. My mother cooked the meals and my grandmother would serve them. My mother was a very good cook. My dad taught her how; he'd learned to cook while working as a houseboy to put himself through dental school."

The midwifery entrance, at the back of the house

DORIS OTAGAKI

GRANDDAUGHTER OF MITO HORI, MIDWIFE

Kuwabara Hospital,
now Issei Memorial Building

"I don't care if they catch me, let them catch me. I've got to fight the fire!" called Nishiura senior to his family as he ran to protect the church.[15]

Kuwabara Hospital's Colonial Revival structure, with its gabled, hipped roof, and grand portico, demonstrates the range of architectural styles and construction techniques in which the Nishiuri Brothers. worked. Built to attract medical practitioners from Japan who would be more sensitive to the community, the facility was named after its first resident doctor, Taisuke Kuwabara, who served as medical director for the hospital's first decade. Prior to the hospital's establishment, Japanese Americans had found that language barriers, along with differences in medical and spiritual practices, prevented them from receiving satisfactory health care from Western-trained doctors.[16] Dr. Kuwabara and succeeding physicians had to return to Japan after working at the hospital, in large part due to continuing discrimination they faced in their profession in the United States. Unable to obtain a California medical license, doctors at Kuwabara Hospital could not perform surgeries and had to be supervised by another local doctor, Dr. James Beattie. Dr. Beattie even held title to the building, due to laws that prohibited Issei from owning property.[17]

Midwives like Mito Hori were able to function with somewhat more autonomy than medical doctors. Although soon to change, childbirth was still viewed as an event best managed by women outside of the medical system. Most Nisei babies were delivered by midwives and Mito Hori's services were in great demand. Hori-san and other midwives provided laboring women and new mothers with reasonably priced, skilled care in a familiar and comforting environment. They spoke the mothers' language and served them carefully prepared Japanese meals for nourishment.[18]

Mito Hori emigrated from Japan with her husband near the turn of the twentieth century. After spending several years working on plantations in Hawaii, they came to San Jose and opened a boarding house in a 1905 bungalow that had served as two classrooms for Grant Elementary School. After purchasing the structures in 1915 and moving them to her 5th Street property, Mrs. Hori soon added her role as midwife and became the family breadwinner.[19] Three generations of the family filled the house: their son-in-law, Dr. Nakahara, practiced dentistry in the front of the house; the family lived in the middle; and the midwifery was located in the rear. Out back, remembered their granddaughter Doris Otagaki, "was grandfather's big flower garden and fish pond. Grandmother made a good living for us."[20]

The midwifery of Mito Hori.

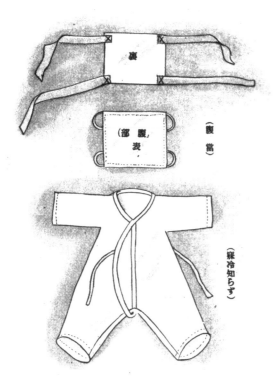

裏

（部腹、
表）

（腹
當）

（痺冷知らず）

Mary Walker Standlee's 1959 study, *The Great Pulse: Japanese Midwifery and Obstetrics through the Ages*, captured some of the traditional Japanese superstitions, beliefs, and cultural practices associated with pregnancy.

Since the Japanese have long been a seafaring people and fish forms a regular part of their diet, many taboos have grown up around this item of food, such as the idea that a hairy child or one with six fingers will be born if crab is eaten during pregnancy. Usually, however, the crab is considered to be a charm against evil and a protection against sickness. Another belief provides that a pregnant woman who harms a crab will bear a child with its characteristics, possibly an oblique forewarning of a child with an ugly disposition…Boneless (soft-boned) children are supposed to develop as a result of eating sea cucumber or octopus. Women in Tottori Prefecture, however, eat octopus to insure curly hair for their offspring. In other places pouring boiling water on an earthworm is considered an easy way to bring about curly-haired children. Clams eaten during the period of gestation will produce tongue-exhibiting children, a naughty habit in any race, but this can be remedied by partaking freely of sparrow and pear, both of which produce short tongues.

TRADITIONAL BELIEFS + PRACTICES

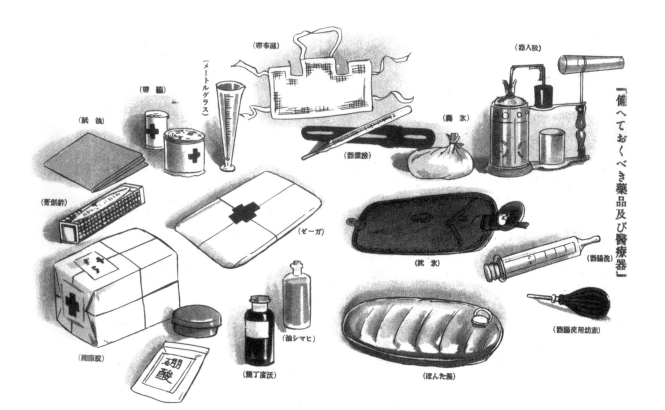

（紙油）
（青絆創）
（綿脂腺）
（帯繃）
（メートルグラス）
（帯布褌）
（器濾旅）
（ゼーガ）
（油シマヒ）
（幾丁度沃）
硼酸
（枕氷）
（ぼんた湯）
（吸入器）
（嚢氷）
「備へておくべき薬品及び醫療器」
（器腸洗）
（器腸洗用坊赤）

Illustrations from the "Infant Nursing Encyclopedia," in the Japanese periodical, *Housewives' Companion*, 1931.

Women from San Jose's Nihonmachi and the outlying farming towns sought out Mito Hori's skills as their families grew. "I remember how grandma kept her hair neatly back and her fingernails cut very short," recalled Doris Otagaki. "The house smelled of Lysol. She always said that cleanliness was very important for her work."[21] Midwives tended their patients from five days to two weeks, caring for mother and newborn and receiving visiting family. San Francisco midwife Kamechiyo Takahashi charged $25 for labor and delivery, and $2 a day for room and board. Recalling that many of her Depression-era clients could not afford the $25 fee, she offered her services anyway because "it was believed in Japan that doctors were to serve people."[22]

Mito Hori ended her midwifery practice and returned to Japan in 1933.[23] The following year, Kuwabara Hospital closed as Japanese American doctors found employment at other local hospitals. However, other health care practitioners continued to operate out of the building; a few years after Mito Hori left San Jose, Mrs. Teranishi rented the second floor for her own midwifery practice.[24]

Determined to keep the building as a vital part of the community, the San Jose Nihonjinkai raised the $5,000 purchase price, which was a substantial sum during the Depression. After moving into a portion of the building, the Nihonjinkai continued to rent offices to doctors and midwives. Dr. Tokio Ishikawa, the first Nisei physician in San Jose, practiced at Kuwabara Hospital in the late 1930s and was a member of the Nisei Service Center, to whom the Nihonjinkai turned over the deed to the building shortly before World War II internment. Such intergenerational transfers of property were a common strategy for thwarting the confiscation of Issei property under the Alien Land Laws.[25]

In the years after internment, the Issei Memorial Building, renamed in 1983, has been home to several important Japanese American social and cultural organizations, including the Japanese American Citizens League, the Japanese American Senior Service Community Center, and the Japanese American Resource Center/Museum, which now resides two doors down in the former home of Dr. Ishikawa at 535 North 5th Street. The building's reincarnation as a hub of community activity is a reflection of the San Jose Nihonmachi's ability to survive and thrive following internment. Unlike Los Angeles's larger Little Tokyo District, which has lost its residential base, San Jose's Japantown still functions as a neighborhood with social, cultural, economic, and residential opportunities for the Japanese American community.[26]

"The hospital was built by some of the Issei, especially from Kumamoto ken, who felt the need to have a hospital where you could have doctors, ...nurses and attendants who could speak Japanese."

Dr. Tokio Ishikawa
Physician at Kuwabara Hospital, 1955

Chapter 9 **LITTLE TOKYO** First Street between San Pedro and Central / **Los Angeles** / California

As children we played on this street and of

Little Tokyo was born quietly in 1885 when a former sailor named Kame, one of perhaps two dozen Japanese in the Los Angeles area, opened a small eatery just off First Street. In the more than one hundred years since, the neighborhood has seen many changes. From its heyday as the largest Japanese enclave in North America, through the dark years of internment and forfeiture, to its renaissance as a center of cultural heritage and pride, Little Tokyo has been a profoundly important place for Japanese Americans of all generations.

At the end of the nineteenth century, a Japanese community was taking shape in Los Angeles. While many of the first immigrants came as wataridori or "birds of passage," a large number chose to stay in the United States and become entrepreneurs and laborers in the booming California economy. Japanese-owned bamboo shops, a tobacco factory, pool halls, dry goods stores, and restaurants appeared throughout Los Angeles, and other Issei began branching out into the rural areas around the city, setting up flower and vegetable farms in the San Gabriel Valley and elsewhere and selling their produce at markets in the city alongside Russian and Chinese immigrants.[1]

Attracted by a new openness between the United States and Japan, thousands of Japanese immigrated to the United States in the first years of the twentieth century, many of them yobiyoshe or "those who were summoned" by relatives already in America. As the Japanese population increased, some white Los Angelenos began to agitate for the exclusion of Japanese from American society. Faced with restrictive immigration laws, exclusionist land policies, and personal hostility, many Issei chose to live in close-knit neighborhoods like the area of the city that was becoming known as Little Tokyo. "You see, the Japanese society then was more like a closed society," recalled Harry Yoshio Ueno, a resident of Little Tokyo. "They couldn't help but live together because a lot of places wouldn't accept them. Landlords wouldn't accept them in renting a house. Because they didn't know a lot of people, they had to live close together."[2] The result was the largest Nihonmachi (Japantown) in America.

James M. Omura remembered Little Tokyo's early years: "[It] wasn't what it is today. It was a jumble of poor establishments and a few nice-looking businesses like the Asia Company, and hotels on both sides, and bigger Nisei-operated pharmacies, like Iwaki Drug and Tenshodo across the street."[3] Forced to the edge of American society and economy, Issei, Kibei, and Nisei of Little

"Japanese society then was more like a closed society. They couldn't help but live together because a lot of places wouldn't accept them. Landlords wouldn't accept them in renting a house. Because they didn't know a lot of people, they had to live close together."

Harry Yoshio Ueno
Little Tokyo resident

FUKUI MORTUARY

One of the oldest Japanese American businesses still in operation in Los Angeles, the Fukui Mortuary has been a Little Tokyo institution for more than eighty years. Its founder, Soji Fukui, was a native of Hiroshima who had also been an entrepreneur in Hawaii, Cleveland, and Seattle. After serving in the 91st Division of the American Expeditionary Forces in France and Belgium during World War I, Fukui's son Hitoshi reunited with his father in Little Tokyo in 1917 and opened the Japanese Undertaking Company in a building that had already served both as a Japanese boarding house and as the Japanese Bethlehem Congregational Church. Over the more than eight decades of its operation, what eventually became known as the Fukui Mortuary has served both Buddhist and, increasingly, Christian members of the community by making space for the Japanese American elements that have become part of both traditions: the gathering of koden (funerary donations), the wearing of black armbands by male family members and helpers at the service, and evening services reminiscent of the days when many Japanese immigrants were laborers by day in the fields and gardens of Los Angeles. Today, the mortuary is owned by Soji's great-grandson Gerald, and continues to be an important Japanese American institution on the city's cultural landscape.

Tokyo created their own world. Although racist legislation in the form of the Exclusion Act barred all immigration from Japan beginning in 1924, for former Little Tokyo resident Sue Kunitomi Embrey, life in Nihonmachi was at least as Japanese as it was American:

My block had a Japanese language school which, I guess, occupied half a block from one end to the other. The rest of the families were Japanese. And across the street there was an old Japanese hospital, and most of the people who lived around there were people who worked in the hospital — nurses and administrators. There was [an] old American Express garage and a factory that made caskets. The rest of the blocks around us, I would say within four or five blocks, were almost all Japanese. We had the only Japanese funeral parlor, the Fukui Mortuary, two blocks away;

Yamato Hall, Little Tokyo, 1939.

the Japanese hospital; the Japanese language school; Amelia Street school; and then on the other side of the grammar school, I think, were some Chinese families and Mexican American families.[4]

A single building in Little Tokyo like Yamato Hall housed a Japanese language newspaper, a martial arts dojo, an auditorium used for meetings and performances, and a gambling club-cum-philanthropic society. Beyond the residents of the neighborhood, Little Tokyo united Japanese from throughout Southern California as Issei and Nisei who lived in smaller enclaves in outlying areas came to the city to connect with family, friends, and homeland through community institutions such as the Hompa Hongwanji Buddhist Temple, founded in 1917 and the Betsuin (head temple) for Southern California. These and other services were crucial links to Japanese culture in an increasingly hostile America.

The 1920s and 1930s have been called Little Tokyo's heyday. In 1941, though, those high times came to an abrupt end with the bombing of Pearl Harbor and the issue of Executive Order 9066. In the name of "national security," the residents of Little Tokyo and other Japanese American communities on the West Coast were given orders to evacuate their homes and businesses. "Depending on where you lived, you were told to be at a particular place by 9 am on a particular day," recounted Little Tokyo resident Amy Uno Ishii. "Then the trucks and buses would roll up and take all your belongings. They tagged everything with your name. Then you got on these trucks and buses. From the minute we left our home to the time we arrived at Santa Anita Racetrack, we had no idea where we were going."[5] They were going to places like Manzanar and Minidoka, sites now synonymous with racist wartime hysteria.

In the absence of their residents and owners, the storefronts and homes of Little Tokyo began to change almost immediately. The wartime

CONFISCATION and EVACUATION

In this 1942 photograph, Los Angeles police officer Joe Aigner inspects garden tools, knives, and shortwave radios confiscated from Japanese Angelenos because of fears they could be used in support of the Japanese army in World War II. When the residents of Little Tokyo and other Japanese American neighborhoods were forced to leave their homes and take only what they could carry to internment camps such as Manzanar, many of their cherished possessions were lost forever. Sometimes, as in the case of Frank Yeizo Nakamura's chef's equipment (brought home after resigning from his job, which he could not get to because of the curfew placed upon Japanese residents), articles were stolen by thieves impersonating government officials. Upon returning from the camps, some Japanese Americans sued for the loss of their possessions. In some cases the Attorney General recognized that Japanese Americans had been forced to dispose of their property under conditions that merited compensation. But many claims were dismissed, like those of Yoshio Bert Shimamaye, who sued for replacement of his shortwave radio, only to learn that since he had given it away for fear of being arrested, he could not be compensated "since such loss was incurred by reason of the claimant's fear of arrest...and not because of his evacuation."

As children we played on this street, and all th

economy attracted thousands of African Americans from the South to the shipyards and munitions factories of Southern California. Restricted from living in white neighborhoods (not unlike their Japanese predecessors) these new migrants from the South established a community of their own in the evacuated neighborhood. When the Japanese internees returned from the camps at the end of the war, they found that Little Tokyo had become part of African American "Bronzeville," a thriving community in its own right.

The former residents of Little Tokyo began the difficult task of reestablishing their community in downtown Los Angeles, which Sue Kunitomi Embrey recalled. "There were still a lot of blacks living in the area, but the small businesses were opening up," she told an interviewer.

I noticed that some of the sushi bars, and places that had been in business, had started up again. Some of the Chinese restaurants that were on First Street were opening up, and so were the markets and grocery stores dealing in Japanese products, but not that many yet. Most of the people that I knew were out in the trailer camps in Burbank, or in Harbor City, which is by the ocean, working in canneries, almost living the same kind of life they had lived in Manzanar, except that they were free to come and go. They could get jobs outside, and a lot of them had their own cars, but it seems that a lot of people were just brought back to Los Angeles by the busloads, and just placed in a lot of these housing areas.[6]

If the wartime internment experience had irrevocably changed the Japanese American community, so also would the postwar prosperity of Los Angeles. In the decades after World War II, Nisei and then Sansei began at last to enjoy the benefits of American citizenship and quickly became participants in the massive suburban development of southern California.[7] As Japanese Americans increasingly made their homes in the outlying communities, Little Tokyo began a slow decline. Some of the Japanese-owned shops that had managed to reopen after the war went out of business, while others were lost to the wrecking ball as financial investment — ironically, much of it from Japan — reshaped the Los Angeles skyline. By the 1980s, much of Little Tokyo was gone except for a core of businesses near the site where Kame had opened his restaurant almost a century earlier, an area now surrounded and dwarfed by the high-rise office towers of multinational corporations.

Frustrated by the loss of their community's heritage, Japanese Americans and other residents of Los Angeles began to come together in the 1980s to discuss ways to preserve the remnants of Little Tokyo. In 1986, the remaining streetscape of buildings on First Street between San Pedro and Central was designated a Historic District and listed on the National Register of Historic Places. The former Hompa Hongwanji Buddhist Temple at the corner of First and Central, named a National Historic Landmark in 1995, is owned by the Japanese American National Museum. The new museum building, across the street, is a haven for the collection and sharing of Nikkei history, made possible by many contributors, including Little Tokyo business owners and a group of highly decorated World War II veterans. And all along the sidewalk of First Street, a public art installation by Sheila de Bretteville reminds visitors of the vibrancy of Little Tokyo: timelines and images etched in the concrete tell of confectioners, florists, priests, tea merchants and other elements of Nihonmachi's heyday. Today, most Japanese American Angelenos live far from Little Tokyo, yet the neighborhood remains as a unique and powerful testament to the ongoing contributions of Japanese Americans to our national heritage.

BOWL

DINING
Coffee Shop
COCKTAILS

THE SANDS

24 HOURS
COFFEE SHOP
BOWLING

photo: Jack Laxer

HOLIDAY BOWL

3730 South Crenshaw Boulevard / **Los Angeles** / California

Built in the Crenshaw District of Los Angeles in 1958, the Holiday Bowl is significant as a landmark to the rise of Nisei bowling and the development of new venues for social life in the postwar period. It was designed by Armet and Davis, the Southern California architects who became known for the Googie style of architecture pioneered by architect John Lautner. This style attracted the masses through an emphasis on signage and bold forms and shapes in building design.[1] It mirrors other automobile oriented architecture of its time such as coffee shops and drive-in theaters.

Japanese Americans took up bowling in the years leading up to World War II, when it was one of the fastest-growing sports in the nation. The large prizes offered by the American Bowling Congress (ABC) in its 1939 and 1940 national championship tournaments drew attention to the sport, garnering new spectators and participants. Prior to the development of automatic pin-spotting machines in the early 1950s, some Nisei youths held jobs as pin boys in neighborhood bowling alleys, where they worked behind the scenes setting pins manually. For some aspiring bowlers, such as the legendary Fuzzy Shimada, this was a dream job during their teen years as it allowed them to hone their skills at a discount during the off hours.[2] But Japanese American entry into the sport, as into the mainstream of American life, was profoundly disrupted by the practice of racial segregation as well as wartime evacuation and internment.

While all could play on an equal footing in what was supposedly "the most democratic sport in the world," not all were acknowledged for their athletic achievements.[3] The ABC formed at the end of the nineteenth century; but it adopted a male-only membership policy in 1906 and amended its constitution to exclude nonwhite members in 1916.[4] The organization refused to sanction teams with nonwhite members or enter the accomplishments of members of unsanctioned teams into the official record, rendering invisible the achievements of women and people of color. The independent National Negro Bowling Association was formed in 1939 for the purpose of enabling its members to develop skill at the game of ten pins through sanctioned league and tournament competition. Similarly, the Nisei leagues arose in response to the racially exclusionary policies of the ABC.

Patrons at the Holiday Bowl, 1997.

The Japanese American Citizen's League (JACL) organized Nisei leagues and tournaments soon after World War II, which allowed Japanese bowlers to play in a circuit of bowling alleys friendly to Japanese American communities, including the Main Bowl in Seattle, the Broadway Bowl in Oakland, the Downtown Bowl in San Francisco, the Fort Street and Fiesta Bowls in San Jose, and the Gardena Bowl and the Holiday Bowl in Los Angeles. Participation in JACL-sponsored tournaments was open to anyone with twenty-five percent or more Japanese ancestry (or by marriage). In many cases, bowling was an extension of relationships established in other walks of life, so the Nisei leagues included the Gardeners' League, the Produce League, the Floral League, and other familiar social environments.[5] Leagues typically were sponsored by Nihonmachi businesses such as banks and florists.[6]

Oral histories of those involved in Nisei bowling explain the process by which young Japanese Americans were drawn into the sport, as well as the meaning it held for the larger community. Mark Fujimoto recalls that Nisei bowling was more of a social activity than a training ground for future professionals, although cash pots upped the ante somewhat. A more ambitious young bowler than most, Mark got the message that:

[Bowling was] great to do on a social level. If you win some money, that's even better. But it's not going to be your career. My dad bowled; he sometimes entered Nisei tournaments. But it's not something that my father took seriously. It was more social, so naturally he wasn't going to make me be serious about it. It was not something for which he was going to shell out money and make me take lessons, as opposed to other things.[7]

Still others recall bowling as an acceptable venue for teen flirtations, in an era when parents were eager to channel their children into marriages with others of their own religion and race. Many Issei parents encouraged their teenagers to participate in the Nisei leagues, since they preferred group activities to the intensity of dating. As Lon Honda remembers,

A lot of it was that everyone did it, like golf is now. I think it was part of our culture, something the Nisei could do. A lot of us — everyone — bowled. [It offered] socializing, [the opportunity to] get

"I think it was part of our culture, something the Nisei could do. A lot of us — everyone — bowled."

Lon Honda
League bowler

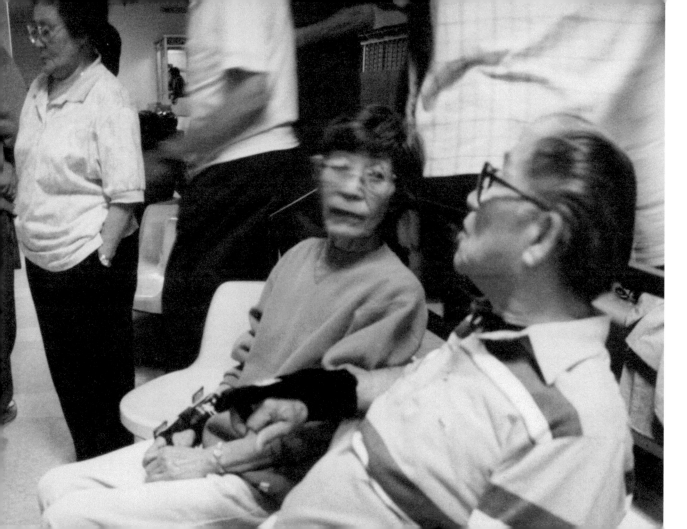

dates, and the competitive piece. All my aunts and uncles were involved through the Buddhist Church. Kids from church wanted to bowl together. There was a strictness about marrying, dating Japanese, [and the message from our parents was] 'Don't lose your culture.' The bowling alley was a safe haven with all thirty or forty lanes of Nisei.[8]

As a person of Hawaiian-Chinese descent, William Apao entered Nisei bowling through marriage. His memories of twice-a-year potlucks held at the local bowling center suggest the importance of food in claiming public spaces for ethnic communities.

You know the Japanese style? Inari, lots of sushi. They had chicken, chow foon, different kinds of foods they eat. Pickled olives. You name it, we had it: salads, cakes, pies. It was just a big feast, you know, twice a year at the lanes. And people used to come down and they were just amazed to see all the different food there. They couldn't get over it. That's one of the things you don't see in a hakujin [Caucasian] league![9]

If the Nisei leagues won the enduring loyalty of bowlers of Japanese descent in the postwar period, it was due to the comfort of socializing and recreating in a familiar community as well as to the harsh reality of racial discrimination. Those who tried to play in white leagues prior to the 1950s were pressured to bow out when the ABC refused to sanction them. Fuzzy Shimada tried to join one such ABC-sanctioned league in Santa Clara, California, only to discover that "If anybody won an ABC award they would not be eligible for it if I was bowling in the league. So I dropped out."[10]

The mid-twentieth century struggle to dismantle racial barriers and win ABC membership meant that the achievements of Japanese Americans,

African Americans, and other bowlers of color would be entered into the historical record. At a time when perfect 300 games were few and far between (the odds against its occurrence were estimated at 300,000 to 1) and excellent bowlers could hope for a perfect game of twelve successive strikes once in a lifetime, the right to official sanction regardless of race was a matter of simple justice.

Seattle played an instrumental role in breaking down racial barriers in bowling through the Boeing Company. As Fuzzy Shimada recalls:

Boeing had some Japanese people working for them and five Japanese bowlers — Nisei bowlers — bowled in the league, and ABC says "No, we won't sanction your league." But Boeing was pretty strong and so eventually it got to where ABC said "Okay, we'll sanction a league for these five Nisei bowlers." Anyway a fellow named Roy Brown, a Seattle sports writer, wrote a lot of articles about it and put pressure on ABC. The following year ABC caved in and let them in the league.[11]

Although men at last were eligible to join the ABC in 1950, and many did, the legacy of racial discrimination left many Japanese Americans more comfortable bowling with family, friends, and neighbors in the Nisei leagues, which continue to the present day under the umbrella of the Japanese American National Bowling Association. Those few Nisei women who dared to dream of turning professional faced yet another obstacle. It would take another forty years before barriers to female membership in the ABC would fall, when in 1993 the "male only" provision finally was removed from its constitution.

Nobu Asami, one of the few Japanese American women who entered the ranks of bowling professionals, came into the sport through the Nisei leagues at the urging of friends.

NOBU ASAMI

"[My husband would] go out early in the morning, golf all day long and come home about 5 o'clock in the evening. So I said 'Geez, this is not working too well, I'm watching the kids all the time and you're out there having fun!' Of course, he works all week, so I said, 'You know, when you come home, you could watch the kids, and I [could go] bowling.' Because bowling was a night thing. And that's what we did. Then he got interested in my bowling, and he kind of took hold of me and coached me. Then he gave up his golf, and then he came with me to all my tournaments… and that's how I [got] started."[12]

FUZZY SHIMADA

"When I was in high school I was a pin boy. In them days they didn't have these automatic pin setters — you used two boys. Well, you only get about 3 cents a line, so it took all night to make 3 dollars. It gave us spending money we could never have gotten."

Born in Vacaville, California, on October 26, 1921, Rokuro "Fuzzy" Shimada moved to San Jose when he was about eleven and eventually went to high school in Santa Clara. He was always involved in athletic activities, but his introduction to bowling came as a pin setter at San Jose's Dolly Bowl, at age eighteen. Two years later, he was placed in an interment camp with other West Coast residents of Japanese descent for the duration of World War II.

After his release from the Heart Mountain camp, he returned to the sport of bowling only to find that racial barriers prevented him from competing at the national level in leagues and tournaments sponsored by the American Bowling Congress (ABC). Nevertheless he amassed an impressive string of victories in Nisei bowling tournaments sponsored by the Japanese American Citizen's League (JACL). He was the only male bowler to win every event at least once in the JACL tournament, becoming the most admired Nisei in the game of bowling. After the ABC lifted its whites-only rule in the early 1950s, Fuzzy participated in ABC national tournaments as well, developing an impressive record. In recent years, ABC recognized his contributions as a pioneer of bowling by inducting him into their Hall of Fame.[13]

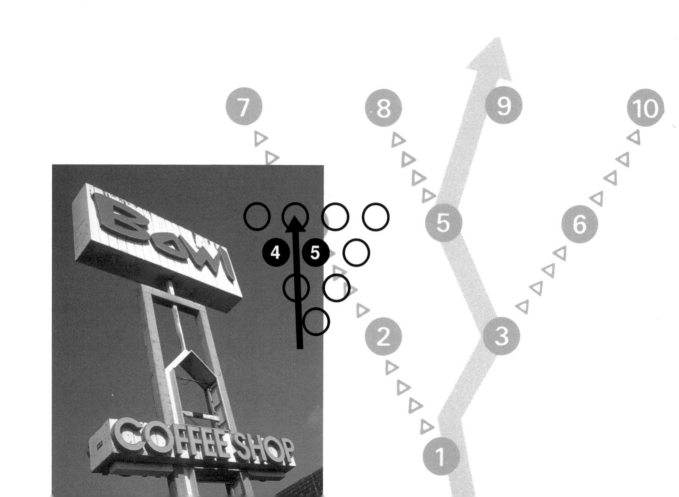

photo: Jack Laxer

The four Japanese American businessmen who developed the Holiday Bowl in 1958 saw an opportunity to own their own property in the Crenshaw area of Los Angeles, build modern lanes with automatic pin spotters, and create a place where people in the community could gather for sport, food, drink, and company. In the 1950s, according to neighborhood history documented in the Crenshaw Neighborhood Plan, second and third-generation Japanese Americans settled into the area between Exposition and King Boulevards immediately east and west of Crenshaw Boulevard, where they built a substantial shopping center. At about the same time, African Americans began their gradual expansion west, out of South Central Los Angeles, through the Jefferson Boulevard, Leimert Park, and Vernon Avenue corridors.[14]

Set in the racially mixed Crenshaw District, the Holiday Bowl brought Japanese American and African American bowlers into close contact with one another, creating some friendships that endured from high school through retirement.

In the late 1960s, effective competition with other Los Angeles bowling alleys required more than multiple lanes and automatic pin spotters to stay in business. Air conditioning, free parking, coffee shops, and supervised nurseries increased

The Holiday Bowl's coffee shop was originally intended to have a Western menu, but the proprietors soon responded to the preferences of its (Japanese American) clientele.

their attractiveness as a source of family recreation, while the ubiquitous billiards room and cocktail lounge promised entertainment more suitable for adults.[15]

The Holiday Bowl's coffee shop was originally intended to have a Western menu, but the proprietors soon responded to the preferences of its clientele, offering Japanese fare instead. This helped them to win the bid to host Nisei bowling tournaments, since the players ate as many as two meals a day in-house.

The Holiday Bowl is remembered by those who participated in the Nisei leagues both for its welcoming Japanese ownership and for the familiar dishes on its coffee shop menu. As Mark Fujimoto recalled, "The food there was [mostly] Japanese and some Chinese. But they had food there that was signature food, I guess you could say, like fried rice or their char siu dishes. That was something you could relate to. And they served green tea."[16]

Lon Honda, who went to the Holiday Bowl for Japanese American National Bowling Association tournaments, noted that the coffee shop "served Spam, sushi, somen, Hawaiian noodle soup (egg, broth, char siu), and rice with their food. When you have that kind of diet, it is the kind of food you want to eat."[17]

In reflecting on his visits to the Holiday Bowl, Lon Honda also noted that "It was the restaurant that I remember. It was not necessarily the greatest, but comfortable to eat two meals a day. When you're at a tournament all day, food is important. You don't want to go on tour and eat hot dogs," which, along with french fries and hamburgers were standard fare in most bowling alley coffee shops.[18]

The Holiday Bowl coffee shop, 1999.

photo: Jack Laxer

NIIGATA

NIIGATA

NAGAOKA

ECHIGO-YUZAWA

FUKUSHIMA

TOCHIGI

GUMMA

Left, the Sakiba. Above, the ceiling of the cocktail lounge.

From the beginning, the Holiday Bowl's cocktail lounge established a playful aesthetic. Known as the Sakiba, its interior, designed by Helen Fong, featured sculptures in the shape of the Japanese Islands hanging from the ceiling. Iconic representations of Japanese prefectures were added to the decor in later years. According to Fong, the choice of a Japanese theme did not reflect a conscious decision to relate the interior design to the building's Japanese ownership or community setting; however, the coincidence acquired significance over the years.[19]

The Nisei bowlers who abstained from alcohol had fewer fond memories of the Sakiba than did the drinkers; however, those who did imbibe argued that it was impossible to separate Nisei bowling from drinking, "as they are married to each other." Mark Fujimoto asserted that "there are even particular drinks that are married to Nisei bowling, including Crown Royal, Chivas, vodka, and beer," particularly beer with ice, due to the Hawaiian influence. So-called sake-bombs or depth-chargers, created by dropping cups of warm sake into cold beer, produced memorable hangovers.[20]

Born in Los Angeles, Helen Fong received professional training in city planning at the University of California, Berkeley, after which she returned to her home town.[18] But at the start of the 1950s, it was difficult for a Chinese American woman to enter the design professions directly, so she started out doing secretarial work in the offices of Gene Choy, which was collocated with Armet and Davis. She gradually learned the ropes of daily architectural practice through typing contracts, handling payment requests, and filing building material catalogues. When Gene Choy's firm downsized, she changed jobs and began working for Armet and Davis, whose practice designing coffee shops was just beginning.

Since Armet and Davis had no background in furnishing restaurants, they went to an equipment house, which would lay out the furnishings and provide plumbing and electrical plans, while the firm designed the color scheme and interior details. Using this process, Armet and Davis carved out a robust practice in the design of coffee shops. The style they used had been pioneered by John Lautner, and it soon gained the moniker "Googie architecture" after one of his clients.

Helen Fong served as the firm's interior designer. It was in this capacity that she designed the interior of the Holiday Bowl as well as the contemporaneous Pann's Restaurant, which became a Los Angeles classic.

Helen retired from the firm at the age of fifty, after more than twenty-five years of employment. Reflecting on the sources of creative inspiration, she laughed and said "that's the question people always ask." What was important to her was that she was having fun, liked her designs, and hoped others would enjoy them too.

HELEN FONG
INTERIOR DESIGNER, SAKIBA AND COFFEE SHOP

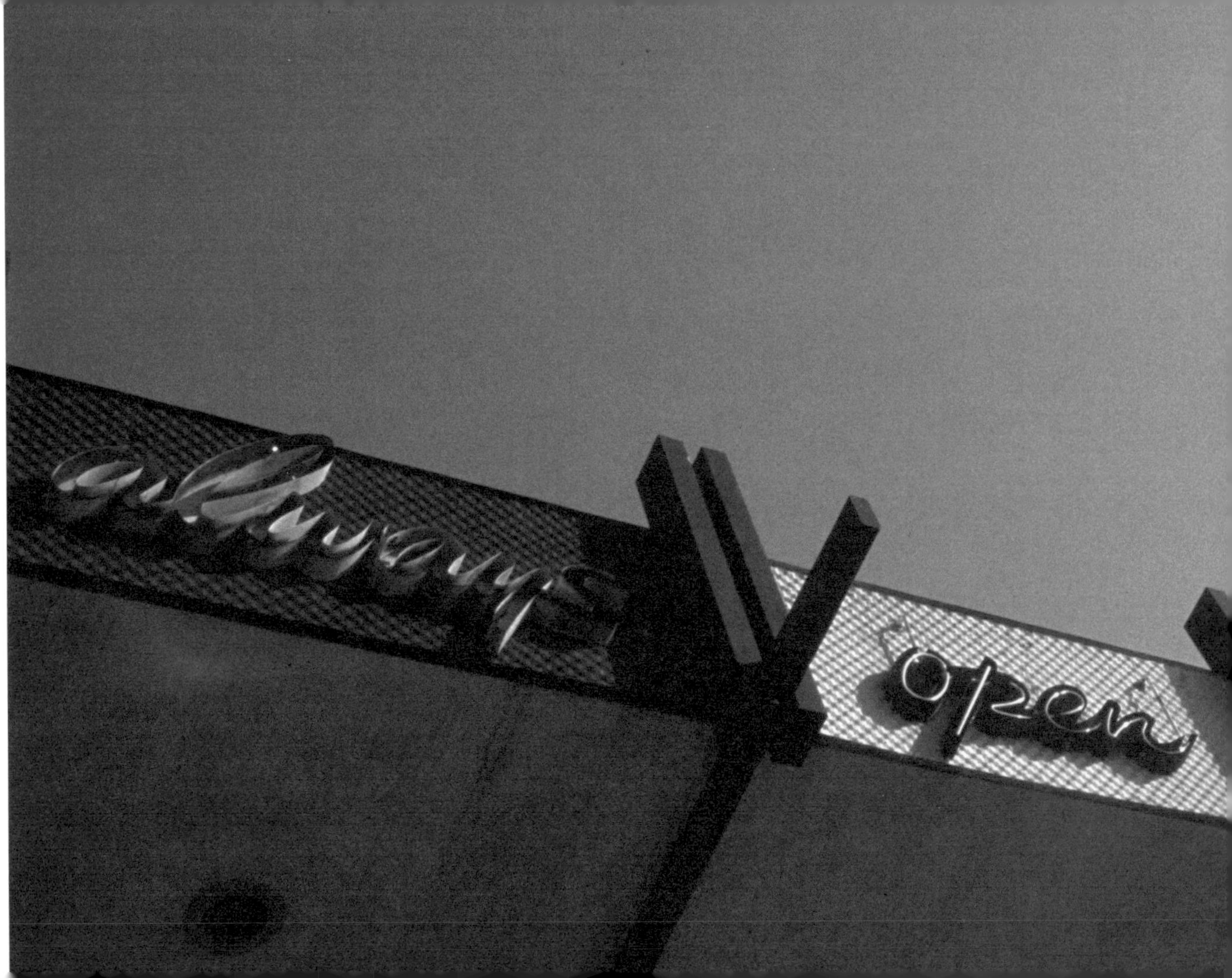
open

The Holiday Bowl quickly became a critical stop on the tournament circuit for Nisei bowlers and home to dozens of Nisei leagues. It remained open twenty-four hours a day for many years, a reflection of the industrial work shift of many of its patrons, particularly those in the aerospace industry. The closing of these plants, the aging of the patrons, and a growing crime rate in the neighborhood eventually led to the introduction of a midnight closing time in the 1980s. Racial tension between the Asian American and African American communities also contributed to its eventual decline in popularity on the Nisei bowling circuit. In addition, the thirty-two lane Holiday Bowl could not effectively compete with new bowling centers that had double the capacity, particularly those in suburban Orange County that were perceived as less threatening venues.

Beginning in 1999, newspaper reports indicated that the Holiday Bowl was threatened with demolition, drawing new attention to its architectural and historical significance at a time when its prospects for remaining in business were diminishing.[21] It ceased operation Sunday, May 7, 2000. In response to public pressure to declare the Holiday Bowl a historic cultural monument, the Los Angeles City Council declared only the coffee shop significant, declining to designate the whole building. Current plans call for redevelopment of the site as a strip mall.

NOTES

Chapter 1: Selleck District

1 U.S. Senate, 61st Congress, 2nd Session. Reports of the Immigration Commission. *Immigrants in Industries*. Part 25: Japanese and Other Immigrant Races in the Pacific Coast and Rocky Mountain States. Japanese and East Indians. (Washington, DC: USGPO, 1911), p. 46.

2 Kazuo Ito, *Issei: A History of Japanese Immigrants in North America*, translated by Shinichiro Nakamura and Jean S. Gerard (Seattle: Japanese Community Service, 1973), p. 313; quoting Isuke Miyazaki of Tokyo.

3 Ronald Olson, *Orientals in the Lumber Industry in the State of Washington* (1928), p. 8.

4 Ito, *Issei*, p. 414.

5 Olson, *Orientals in the Lumber Industry*, p. 16.

6 Bradley Bowden and Lynn L. Larson, *Cultural Resources Assessment Japanese Camp and Lavender Town, Selleck, King County, Washington* (Seattle: King County Cultural Resources Division, 1997), p. 11; citing Ed Suguro, "Old Sawmill Town Remembered," *Northwest Nikkei* (May 1994): 7, 15.

7 Bowden and Larson, *Cultural Resource Assessment Japanese Camp*, p. 8.

8 Ito, *Issei*, p. 313.

9 Ito, *Issei*, pp. 402-403.

10 Suguro, "Old Sawmill Town Remembered," 7, 15.

11 Bowden and Larson, *Cultural Resource Assessment Japanese Camp*, p. 26.

Chapter 2: Neely Mansion

1 *History of the Neely Mansion* collected by Fred Hardin (Auburn, Washington: n.p., 1982).

2 Mary Mendenhall, "The Neely Mansion," King County Register of Historic Places - Nomination Form (Seattle: King County Office of Historic Preservation, 1982).

3 The rough outlines of the Neely Mansion's history were explained by Linda Van Nest in a 1994 interview. Thereafter, she has provided occasional updates.

4 Mimi Sheridan et al, "The Neely Mansion: Connections to the Asian/Pacific American Community." Unpublished paper prepared for a graduate seminar in historic preservation at the University of Washington. Prepared for King County under the supervision of Gail Dubrow (Seattle: University of Washington, Preservation Planning and Design Program, 1995).

5 Mildred T. Andrews, "The Hori Furo," King County Landmark Registration Form (Seattle: King County Cultural Resources Division, 1996).

6 See, for example, Peggy Ziebarth, "Neely Mansion," *Valley Daily News* (June 12, 1994).

7 John Isao Nishinoiri, "Japanese Farms in Washington" (MA thesis, University of Washington, 1926).

8 Sheridan et al, "The Neely Mansion."

9 Kazuo Ito, *Issei: A History of Japanese Immigrants in North America*, translated by Shinichiro Nakamura and Jean S. Gerard (Seattle: Japanese Community Service, 1973), p. 476.

10 Ito, *Issei*, p. 476.

11 Ito, *Issei*, pp. 475-476.

12 This description of the milker's workday is drawn from Otoshi's account in Ito, *Issei*, p. 475.

13 Ito, *Issei*, p. 477.

14 Stacy Patterson interviewed June Acosta on April 11 and April 25, 1994.

15 Most of the information about the condition of the Neely property during and after World War II came from Pedro (Pete) Acosta, who was interviewed by University of Washington graduate students in Preservation Planning and Design on April 24, 1994.

Chapter 3: Natsuhara's Store

1 Wini Carter, "Pioneer Grocers: Natsuharas' Store Has Changed Little in 65 Years," *Daily News Journal* (November 13, 1980).

2 "Auburn Business Fire Leaves a Family's Heritage in Ashes," *Seattle Post-Intelligencer* (August 20, 1999), p. B1; and "Auburn Fire Work of an Arsonist," *Seattle Post-Intelligencer* (August 21, 1999), p. B1.

3 Kazuo Ito, *Issei: A History of Japanese Immigrants in North America*, translated by Shinichiro Nakamura and Jean S. Gerard (Seattle: Japanese Community Service, 1973), p. 192.

4 Ito, *Issei*, p. 192.

5   According to her account in Ito, *Issei*, pp. 193-194, after a wedding ceremony in Japan and fourteen months of legal wrangling, Sen set sail for Seattle, enduring the pain of separation from her family and violent seasickness. Her ship, the *Kamikawa Maru*, docked at Smith's Cove on June 1, but it was several days before the four picture brides on board were allowed to land because they lacked U.S. marriage licenses. They therefore arranged for a marriage ceremony to be held on the boat with their new husbands. Unable to speak a word of English, Sen could only presume that the presiding minister was wishing them well. Thus she began married life.

6   Ito, *Issei*, p. 194.

7   Ito, *Issei*, p. 194.

8   Carter, "Pioneer Grocers."

9   "Auburn People Get Rice Direct," *Auburn Globe* (April 25, 1914). Also recounted by Frank Natsuhara.

10 *Japanese Immigration: Hearings Before the Committee on Immigration and Naturalization*, House of Representatives, 66th Congress, 2nd Session (July 12, 13, and 14, 1920). Parts 1 and 2 (Washington, DC: USGPO, 1921). Part 4 (July 26, 27, 28, 29, 1920) is particularly relevant since hearings were held in Seattle and Tacoma, Washington.

11 *Auburn Globe Republican* (December 8, 1922).

12 Ito, *Issei*, p. 128.

13 Ito, *Issei*, p. 175.

14 References to members of the local Japanese community being killed on the tracks are found in *Auburn Globe* (July 22, 1915); *Auburn Globe Republican* (December 19, 1919); *Auburn Globe Republican* (December 14, 1921); *Auburn Globe Republican* (October 14, 1921).

15 *Auburn Globe Republican* (February 20, 1942).

16 *Auburn Globe Republican* (April 24, 1942).

17 *Auburn Globe Republican* (May 22, 1942).

18 Frank had to meet Sonnemann in Pasco (in eastern Washington State) to talk about it. Among the wreckage was an overturned urn, leaving ashes scattered inside their home. The defilement was deeply troubling, but it also represented something of a dilemma. Since the ashes did not belong to anyone the Natsuhara family knew, they were puzzled about where they had come from or what they should do with them.

19 They would not have sold the property had they known the war was about to end. So too, the internment camp administrators failed to process the paperwork in a sufficiently timely way to reverse the transaction when the war ended a few days later.

20 The original façade remained in place behind it. It was visible only when looking outward, a view only the family saw.

21 Frank and his wife, Shizuko, originally lived on the ground floor, behind the kitchen area. Only when the rest of the family moved out did they make the upstairs apartment their home.

22 Chiyokichi Natsuhara was so diligent in his care of the cemetery that he regularly sent money from the internment camp to someone who looked after it. Frank took up this responsibility after his father's death and spearheaded the campaign for the cemetery's acquisition by the Parks Department to address long-term maintenance and protection concerns.

Chapter 4: Nippon Kan Hall

1 Interview with Tama Tokuda by Gail Dubrow (May 28, 1997).

2 Interview with Tama Tokuda (May 28, 1997). For more on how the hana system operated at Nippon Kan, see Kikuyo Murata of Seattle in Kazuo Ito, *Issei: A History of Japanese Immigrants in North America*, translated by Shinichiro Nakamura and Jean S. Gerard (Seattle: Japanese Community Service, 1973), pp. 803-804.

3 Interview with Tama Tokuda (May 28, 1997).

4 Budd Fukei, *The Japanese American Story* (Minneapolis: Dillon Press, 1976), pp. 122-123.

5 This description is drawn from an interview with Tama Tokuda and a description provided by Fukei, *The Japanese American Story*, p. 124.

6 Minoru Masuda, Ph.D., Professor, Department of Psychiatry and Behavioral Sciences, University of Washington, to the State Advisory Council on Historic Preservation, in support of the listing of Nippon Kan Hall on the National Register of Historic Places (November 2, 1977).

7 David A. Rash, *The Asian American Presence in Seattle* (Unpublished Manuscript, 1998), p. 17. Rash has documented the design and construction of many of Seattle's Nihonmachi buildings. He generously shared his unpublished paper, which jump-started this research on the Japanese Language School and Nippon Kan Hall.

8   *Seattle Times* (September 24, 1905), p. 8.

9   Rash, *The Asian American Presence in Seattle*, p. 17.

10 Rash, *The Asian American Presence in Seattle*, p. 17.

11 Rash, *The Asian American Presence in Seattle*, p. 18.

12 Fukei, *The Japanese American Story*, p. 122.

13 T. Philip Terry, *Terry's Guide to the Japanese Empire* (Boston: Houghton Mifflin, 1927), p. 116.

14 Ito, *Issei*, pp. 803-804.

15 Gensaburo Ohashi of Seattle, quoted in Ito, *Issei*, p. 816.

16 Ohashi of Seattle, quoted in Ito, *Issei*, p. 817.

17 Interview with Tama Tokuda (May 28, 1997).

18 Miyoshi Yorita of Seattle, quoted in Ito, *Issei*, p. 801.

19 Monica Sone, *Nisei Daughter* (Seattle: University of Washington Press, 1991), pp. 45-46. Originally published by Atlantic Monthly Press, 1953.

20 Sone, *Nisei Daughter*, p. 66.

21 Sone, *Nisei Daughter*, p. 70.

22 Edward M. Burke, "Rebirth of the Nippon Kan," *Puget Soundings* (February 1984), pp. 26-28.

Chapter 5: Hashidate-Yu

1   Peter Grilli and Dana Levy, *Pleasures of the Japanese Bath* (New York: Weatherhill, 1992), p. 57.

2   Kazuo Ito, *Issei: A History of Japanese Immigrants in North America*, translated by Shinichiro Nakamura and Jean S. Gerard (Seattle: Japanese Community Service, 1973), p. 522.

3   Dell Uchida, *Remembering the Ofuro [Japanese Public Baths]* (Japanese Heritage Historical Society, 1993).

4   Interview with Edward Sano by Gail Dubrow (January 16, 1999).

5   Uchida, *Remembering the Ofuro*.

6   Mas Fukuhara, unpublished reminiscence, distributed as a handout on the occasion of a public tour of Hashidate-Yu (n.d.).

7   Interview with Edward Sano (January 16, 1999).

8   Fukuhara, unpublished reminiscence.

9   Interview with Edward Sano (January 16, 1999).

10 Interview with Edward Sano (January 16, 1999).

11 Ito, *Issei*, p. 861.

12 *Rafu Shimpo* (Los Angeles: Rafu Shimpo, 1939), p. 95.

13 *Rafu Shimpo*, pp. 465 and 471.

14 *Rafu Shimpo*, p. 506.

15 Interview with Edward Sano (January 16, 1999).

16 Ito, *Issei*, p. 866.

17 Ito, *Issei*, p. 823.

18 Ito, *Issei*, pp. 840-841.

19 Fukuhara, unpublished reminiscence.

20 Akemi Kikumura, *Through Harsh Winters: The Life of a Japanese Immigrant Woman* (Novato, CA: Chandler & Sharp, 1981), p. 9.

Chapter 6: Kokugo Gakko

1 Yoriaki Nakagawa, *Nichi-Bei Sahlo No Jloshiki/ The Common Sense of Japanese and American Etiquette* (Tokyo: Ueda Shoten, 1937).

2 As Nakagawa clearly articulated in *The Common Sense of Japanese and American Etiquette*, "I used this [book] as a teaching material for the study of both language and etiquette."

3 Bill Hosokawa, *Nisei: The Quiet Americans* (New York: William Morrow, 1969), p. 159.

4 Toyotomi Morimoto, *Japanese Americans and Cultural Continuity: Maintaining Language and Heritage* (New York: Garland, 1997), p. 72.

5 *Seattle Times* (September 24, 1905), p. 8.

6 *Seattle Times* (August 17, 1905), p. 3.

7 *Seattle Times* (September 24, 1905), p. 8.

8 *Seattle Times* (June 30, 1908).

9 Yuji Ichioka, *The Issei: The World of the First Generation Japanese Immigrants, 1885-1924* (New York: The Free Press, 1988), pp. 198-199.

10 National Register Inventory - Nomination Form, "Kokugo Gakko or Seattle Japanese Language School."

11   Ichioka, *The Issei*, pp. 196-210.

12   Hosokawa, *Nisei*, p. 172.

13   Group interview with former Kokugo Gakko pupils, St. Peter's Episcopal Church, Seattle, Washington, by Gail Dubrow (June 19, 1997).

14   Group interview with former Kokugo Gakko pupils (June 19, 1997).

15. Interview with Sam Shoji by Gail Dubrow (May 13, 1997).

16   Kazuo Ito, *Issei: A History of Japanese Immigrants in North America*, translated by Shinichiro Nakamura and Jean S. Gerard (Seattle: Japanese Community Service, 1973), p. 597. This incident dates to the 1928-30 period.

17   Group interview with former Kokugo Gakko pupils (June 19, 1997).

18   Group interview with former Kokugo Gakko pupils (June 19, 1997).

19   Group interview with former Kokugo Gakko pupils (June 19, 1997).

20   "Picnic Shows There Are Many Japanese: South Park Residents Wonder Where All of the 2,000 Brown Men Who Met There Sunday Came From," *Seattle Times* (March 17, 1908), p. 12.

21   Ito, *Issei*, p. 97.

22   Interview with Sam Shoji (May 13, 1997).

23   An October 27, 1997 reunion of former residents was was documented by the Densho Project of Seattle. Also see Lily Eng, "Bittersweet Journey Back to Their Past," *Seattle Times* (October 27, 1997), p. B1.

Chapter 7: Enmanji Temple

 1   Tetsuden Kashima, *Buddhism in America* (Westport, CT: Greenwood Press, 1977), pp. 3-5.

 2   Gail Dubrow and Lisa Raflo, "Draft Historic Context on Buddhist Churches and Temples," in Gail Dubrow et al, *National Study of Japanese American Cultural Resources* (Seattle: Preservation Planning and Design Program, University of Washington, 1999), p. 6.

 3   Dubrow and Raflo, "Draft Historic Context On Buddhist Churches and Temples," p. 10; citing Kashima, *Buddhism in America*, pp. 13-16, 23.

 4   Dubrow and Raflo, "Draft Historic Context on Buddhist Churches and Temples," pp. 9-10; citing Kashima, *Buddhism in America*, p. 21.

5   Kashima, *Buddhism in America*, p. 16.

6   Dubrow and Raflo, "Draft Historic Context on Buddhist Churches and Temples," pp. 8-9.

7   Dubrow and Raflo, "Draft Historic Context on Buddhist Churches and Temples," p. 16.

8   Kashima, *Buddhism in America*, p. 36.

9   *Buddhist Churches of America, Volume 1: 75 Year History, 1899-1974* (Chicago: Nobart, Inc., 1974), p. 358.

10 *Buddhist Churches of America, Volume 1: 75 Year History, 1899-1974* (Chicago: Nobart, Inc., 1974), p. 358.

11 Jeannie Yang, "Enmanji Temple," National Register of Historic Places Registration Form (Sonoma, CA: Anthropological Studies Center, Sonoma State University, 1995), p. 2.

12 Clay Lancaster, *The Japanese Influence in America* (New York: Abbeville Press, 1983), pp. 51-62.

13 Lancaster, *The Japanese Influence in America*, pp. 77-83.

14 *Enmanji Buddhist Temple* (Sebastopol, CA: Enmanji Buddhist Temple, n.d.), p. 3.

15 Yang, "Enmanji Temple," p. 2.

16 *Buddhist Churches of America*, p. 358.

17 Interview with Yoneko "Pat" Shimizu by Donna Graves (July 1997).

18 Interview with Minoru Matsuda by Donna Graves (July 1997).

19 Yang, "Enmanji Temple," p. 4.

20 Yang, "Enmanji Temple," pp. 5-6.

21 *Buddhist Churches of America*, p. 359.

22 Dubrow and Raflo, "Draft Historic Context on Buddhist Churches and Temples," p. 17.

23 Kashima, *Buddhism in America*, pp. 41-42. Conversations with Zen practitioners Alan and Laurie Senauke helped to distinguish between the architecture of zendo and other Buddhist structures.

24 *Buddhist Churches of America*, p. 357.

Chapter 8: Kuwabara Hospital and Midwifery

1   Kazuo Ito, *Issei: A History of Japanese Immigrants in North America*, translated by Shinichiro Nakamura and Jean S. Gerard (Seattle: Japanese Community Service, 1973), p. 252.

2   Ito, *Issei*, p. 250.

3   Ito, *Issei*, p. 261.

4   Ito, *Issei*, p. 576.

5   Ito, *Issei*, pp. 583-584.

6   Ito, *Issei*, p. 580.

7   Ito, *Issei*, p. 582.

8   Ito, *Issei*, p. 580.

9   Ito, *Issei*, p. 581.

10   Ito, *Issei*, p. 583.

11   Ito, *Issei*, p. 581.

12   Ito, *Issei*, p. 584.

13   "Kuwabara Hospital," Historic Resources Inventory Form (Sacramento: California Department of Parks and Recreation, 1979), p. 2.

14   Steven Misawa, editor, *Beginnings: Japanese Americans in San Jose* (San Jose: San Jose Japanese American Community Senior Service Center, 1981), p. 85. "A Guide to San Jose's Historic Japantown Open House" (San Jose: Preservation Action Council of San Jose, 1992).

15   Misawa, ed., *Beginnings*, p. 86.

16   "A Guide to San Jose's Historic Japantown Open House."

17   "Kuwabara Hospital," p.2.

18   "Midwifery," Historic Resources Inventory Form (Sacramento: California Department of Parks and Recreation, 1979), p. 2. Telephone interview with Doris Otagaki by Donna Graves (February 1998).

19   "A Guide to San Jose's Historic Japantown Open House."

20   Interview with Doris Otagaki (February 1998).

21   Interview with Doris Otagaki (February 1998).

22   Oral history with Kamechiyo Takahashi in *The Issei: Portrait of a Pioneer; An Oral History*, edited by Eileen Sunada Sarasohn (Palo Alto: Pacific Books, 1983), p. 99.

23   Interview with Doris Otagaki (February 1998).

24   "A Guide to San Jose's Historic Japantown Open House."

25   "Kuwabara Hospital," p. 3.

26 "Kuwabara Hospital," p. 3.

Chapter 9: Little Tokyo

1 William M. Mason and John A. McKinstry, *The Japanese of Los Angeles* (Los Angeles: Los Angeles County Museum, 1969); John Modell, *The Economics and Politics of Racial Accommodation: The Japanese of Los Angeles, 1900-1942* (Urbana: University of Illinois Press, 1977), pp. 26-27; Ronald Takaki, *Strangers From a Different Shore: A History of Asian Americans* (New York: Penguin Books, 1989), p. 193.

2 *Japanese American World War II Evacuation Oral History Project*, Part 4, Arthur A. Hansen, ed., (Westport, Conn.: Meckler Publishing, 1991), p. 10.

3 *Japanese American World War II Evacuation Oral History Project*, Part 4, Hansen, ed., p. 206.

4 *Japanese American World War II Evacuation Oral History Project*, Part 1, Hansen, ed., p. 102.

5 *Japanese American World War II Evacuation Oral History Project*, Part 1, Hansen, ed., p. 64.

6 *Japanese American World War II Evacuation Oral History Project*, Part 1, Hansen, ed., p. 139.

7 Roger Daniels, *Asian America: Chinese and Japanese in the United States Since 1850* (Seattle: University of Washington Press, 1988), p. 294.

Chapter 10: Holiday Bowl

1 Alan Hess, *Googie: Fifties Coffee Shop Architecture* (San Francisco: Chronicle Books, 1985).

2 Interview with Fuzzy Shimada by Gail Dubrow (February 1, 1999).

3 Joe Falcaro, *Bowling For All* (New York: Ronald Press, 1957), p. 5.

4 <http://members.aol.com/bowlerweb/history/htm>.

5 Peter Y. Hong, "Another Kind of Holiday Bowl Tradition," *Los Angeles Times* (February 2, 1996), pp. B1, B8.

6 Interview with William Apao by Gail Dubrow (February 1, 1999).

7 Interview with Mark Fujimoto by Gail Dubrow (January 22, 1999).

8 Correspondence from Lon Honda to Gail Dubrow (February, 1999).

9 Interview with William Apao (February 1, 1999).

10 Interview with Fuzzy Shimada (February 1, 1999).

11 Interview with Fuzzy Shimada (February 1, 1999).

12 Interview with Nobu Asami by Gail Dubrow (February 1, 1999).

13 Interview with Fuzzy Shimada (February 1, 1999). Biographical information on Rokuro "Fuzzy" Shimada was also drawn from his Hall of Fame nomination, prepared by William Apao.

14 "Crenshaw Neighborhood Plan: Community Profile," <http://crenshaw.org/CN_2/CNPlan2.htm>, p. 4.

15 John English researched bowling alley advertisements from the 1940s and 1950s in the *Los Angeles Times* and Los Angeles directories.

16 Interview with Mark Fujimoto (January 22, 1999).

17 Interview with Lon Honda by Gail Dubrow (February 1999).

18 Interview with Lon Honda (February 1999).

19 Interviews with Helen Fong conducted by Donna Graves and Eugenia Woo at the Holiday Bowl, 1997.

20 Interview with Mark Fujimoto (January 22, 1999).

21 Ed Leibowitz, "Holiday Bowl: Strike or Spare?" *Los Angeles Times Magazine* (August 8, 1999), p. 8. John English generously provided an update on the status of the Holiday Bowl in March 2002.

PHOTO CREDITS

Cover

Mark Edward Harris, photographer (1999).

Introduction

Karen Cheng, photographer (2000).

Chapter 1: Selleck District

6   Asian choke setters under boom loader, Oregon and American Lumber Company, n.d.
     Clark Kinsey, photographer. MSCUA, University of Washington Libraries, C. Kinsey 2503.

8   Gail Dubrow, photographer.

9   Courtesy of Kiyo Maekawa.

10   MSCUA, University of Washington Libraries, UW6956.

12   Courtesy of Kiyo Maekawa.

14   Clark Kinsey, photographer. MSCUA, University of Washington Libraries, C. Kinsey 999.

16   Reproduced from Bradley Bowden and Lynn L. Larson, *Cultural Resources Assessment Japanese
     Camp and Lavender Town, Selleck, King County, Washington* (Seattle: King County Cultural
     Resources Division, 1997), p. 13.
     This school house photo originally appeared in Kojiro-cho Takeuchi, *Beikoku Seihokubo Nihon
     Imin Shi* (Shiatoru-shi: Taihoku Nipposha, 1929).

17   Above, Japanese Camp, from Kazuo Ito, *Issei: A History of Japanese Immigrants in North
     America*, translated by Shinichiro Nakamura and Jean S. Gerard (Seattle: Japanese Community
     Service, 1973), p. 410.
     Below, housing for white workers, Mary Woodman, photographer.

18   Courtesy of Frank Natsuhara.

20   Courtesy of Professor Gerald Hedlund, Green River Community College.

22   Courtesy of Kiyo Maekawa.

92   Courtesy of Edward Sano.

93   Courtesy of Edward Sano.

96   Washington State Archives, Puget Sound Branch, King County Assessor's Property Record Cards.

98   Courtesy of Frank Ching.

99   Todd Maggio, photographer (2001).

100   Todd Maggio, photographer (2001).

102   Gail Dubrow, photographer.

Chapter 6: Kokugo Gakko

104   Kokugo Gakko picnic at Alki Point (June 3, 1912), MSCUA, University of Washington Libraries, UW6314.

106   From Yoriaki Nakagawa, *Nichi-Bei Sahlo No Jloshiki/Common Sense of Japanese and American Etiquette* (Tokyo: Uedaya Shoten, 1937), p. 13.

107   Broadway Evening School (1917). Seattle Public Schools Archives.

108   From left to right, Nakagawa, *Nichi-Bei Sahlo No Jloshiki/Common Sense of Japanese and American Etiquette*, p. 63

109   From left to right, Nakagawa, *Nichi-Bei Sahlo No Jloshiki/Common Sense of Japanese and American Etiquette*, pp. 145 and 173.

110   From left to right, Nakagawa, *Nichi-Bei Sahlo No Jloshiki/Common Sense of Japanese and American Etiquette*, pp. 85 and 159.

111   From left to right, Nakagawa, *Nichi-Bei Sahlo No Jloshiki/Common Sense of Japanese and American Etiquette*, pp. 82, and 88.

112   From *North American Times Yearbook* (1936).

113   Above, MSCUA, University of Washington Libraries, AYP 062. Below, Seattle Buddhist Temple Archives.

114   From left to right, Nakagawa, *Nichi-Bei Sahlo No Jloshiki/Common Sense of Japanese and American Etiquette*, pp. 178 and 75.

115   From left to right, Nakagawa, *Nichi-Bei Sahlo No Jloshiki/Common Sense of Japanese and American Etiquette*, p. 222.

116   MSCUA, University of Washington Libraries, Matsushita Collection 162, Box 10, Folder 17.

118   Courtesy of Henry Itoi and Monica Itoi Sone.

120   Courtesy of Alice M. Kawanishi.

122   Seattle Buddhist Temple Archives.

124   John Stamets, photographer (1997).

Chapter 7: Enmanji Buddhist Temple

126   Dedication Service (April 15, 1934). Courtesy of Reverend Carol Himaka, Enmanji Buddhist Temple.

128   *Buddhist Churches of America, Volume 1. 75 Year History, 1899-1974* (Chicago: Hobart, 1974), p. 362.

129   From left to right: *Buddhist Churches of America, Volume 1. 75 Year History, 1899-1974* (Chicago: Hobart, 1974), pp. 213 and 396.

131   Courtesy of Reverend Carol Himaka, Enmanji Buddhist Temple.

133   Courtesy of Reverend Carol Himaka, Enmanji Buddhist Temple.

134   Courtesy of Reverend Carol Himaka, Enmanji Buddhist Temple.

135   Courtesy of Reverend Carol Himaka, Enmanji Buddhist Temple.

136   All images *NikkeiWest*. Jeffrey Kimoto, photographer (2001).

137   Seattle Buddhist Temple Archives.

138   Courtesy of Reverend Carol Himaka, Enmanji Buddhist Temple.

139   Donna Graves, photographer.

Chapter 8: Kuwabara Hospital and Midwifery

140   From Kago Katayama, *Bei Ka Shussho Nihon Jido/U.S. and Canadian-Born Japanese Children* (Tokyo: Shinyodo Publishing Company, 1918). This book covers Vancouver, Seattle, Eastern Washington, and Portland. Courtesy of Takashi and Lily Hori.

142   Katayama, *Bei Ka Shussho Nihon Jido/U.S. and Canadian-Born Japanese Children.*

143   Katayama, *Bei Ka Shussho Nihon Jido/U.S. and Canadian-Born Japanese Children.*

144   Katayama, *Bei Ka Shussho Nihon Jido/U.S. and Canadian-Born Japanese Children.*

147   From Masahiro Shiraki, *Juken You Josanpu Gaku/Reference Book of Midwifery* (Tokyo: Nanzan Dou, 1927). Collection of the National Library of Medicine. Translation courtesy of Takahiro Abe.

Chapter 10: Holiday Bowl

174   Jack Laxer, photographer.

176   Richard Ross, photographer (1997).

178   Richard Ross, photographer (1997).

180   Richard Ross, photographer (1997).

183   Cartoon from *Hokubei Mainichi* (July 28. 1960). Courtesy of Nobu Asami.

184   Todd Maggio, photographer (2001).

186   Todd Maggio, photographer (2001). Diagrams from Chuck Pezzano and Herm Weiskopf, *Sports Illustrated Bowling* (New York: Harper and Row, 1981), p. 98.

187   Jack Laxer, photographer.

188   Todd Maggio, photographer (2001).

189   Eugenia Woo, photographer (1999).

190   Jack Laxer, photographer.

191   Eugenia Woo, photographer (1999).

192   Left, Todd Maggio, photographer (2001). Right, Eugenia Woo, photographer (1999).

193   Courtesy of Helen Ming Fong.

194   Todd Maggio, photographer (2001).

ACKNOWLEDGMENTS

Sento at Sixth and Main was developed with major support from Seattle City Light Percent for Art Funds, administered by the Seattle Arts Commission. SAC's Urban Collaborations Program invited artists to propose projects and collaborations on sites of their own choosing. Deepest thanks go to Marcia Iwasaki, Project Manager, and Barbara Goldstein, Director of Public and Community Arts at the Seattle Arts Commission, who steadfastly supported the collaboration with Japanese American communities that evolved over the course of this project. Bea Kiyohara, who served as a SAC Commissioner, also deserves credit for helping to launch the project in the Seattle community. Pat Soden and Naomi B. Pascal were instrumental in the decision of UW Press to take on the book's distribution.

Several other funders provided publication support: the Graham Foundation for Advanced Studies in the Fine Arts, the Simpson Center for the Humanities and the Harry Bridges Center for Labor Studies at the University of Washington, and the Motoda Foundation of Seattle. Roberta Feldman and Jan Kumasaka generously shared their connections to funding sources at a critical moment in the project's history. Kathleen Woodward and Margit Dementi have been particularly enthusiastic supporters whose understanding of the interdisciplinary and collaborative nature of this work was most welcome. Jerry Finrow and Bob Mugerauer provided a climate of support for this work as in their role at the helm of the College of Architecture and Urban Planning at the University of Washington.

Dolores Hayden's Power of Place Project served as an important model for documenting neglected aspects of the built environment and cultural landscape, and making them publicly visible. This book builds upon her work. It is also the culmination of a decade of research on the preservation of Asian American heritage undertaken through the Preservation Planning and Design Program at the University of Washington. Related projects were supported at various times by the National Park Service, the Washington State Office of Archaeology & Historic Preservation, and the King County Office of Cultural Resources, among other agencies. Important advocates for this work include Carol Shull, Dwight Pitcaithley, Heather Huyck, John Sprinkle, Antoinette Lee, Eugene Itogawa, Neil King, John Reynolds, Stephanie Toothman, Gretchen Luxenberg, Rob Harbour, Jerry Takano, Charles Payton, Julie Koler, Leonard Garfield, Jennifer Meisner, and Eugenia Woo, among other colleagues in the preservation community who are dedicated to protecting cultural resources reflective of the nation's diversity.

All praise is due to designer Karen Cheng, who turned the mountains of material generated by this project into an elegant form. In addition to Donna Graves' contributions to the book as author of the Kuwabara Hospital/Midwifery and Enmanji Buddhist Temple chapters, her expertise as a cultural planner shaped and strengthened the project. The book has benefited visually from original photography by Todd Maggio, Richard Ross, and John Stamets. It is an added pleasure to be able to include the work of Mark Edward Harris and Jack Laxer.

Three artists involved in earlier stages of the project deserve thanks and apologies: Judy Anderson, Frank Ching and Kim Yasuda. I regret being unable to include their original artwork in the book, but remain grateful for their contributions to conceptualizing the project. Judy Anderson's work on proposals, involvement in early stages of book design and securing donations-in-kind merit a special note of gratitude.

Coll-Peter Thrush and Eugenia Woo made original contributions not credited on the cover. Coll-Peter Thrush is the principal author of the chapter on Little Tokyo. Eugenia Woo co-authored the chapter on the Holiday Bowl, which including research by Donna Graves and John English. Connie Walker co-authored a related National Historic Landmark nomination on Hashidate-Yu that generated much new information; Carol Bushar, Jade Takashima, and Barbara Smith-Steiner have worked on the NHL nomination for Nippon Kan Hall.

Research assistance from Kathleen Kern, Coll-Peter Thrush, and Brian Casserly moved the project forward. Matt Emery's help was critical in recording the Natsuhara-Maekawa interview on video. Patricia Iolavera, Kathleen Kern, and Andrea Masotti provided transcripts of the oral histories, while Nazila Merati worked extensively with Japanese American city directories. Takahiro Abe provided translations from Japanese to English. A special thanks to those who did this work; it was tedious at times, but important in the overall scheme of things.

Able editors Nancy Crowley, Mary Hutchins, Neile Graham, and Brian Casserly vastly improved the manuscript. I would like to express my appreciation as well to those who kindly agreed to review all or part of the book while in draft form. Many errors of grammar, fact and interpretation were discovered thanks to Mildred Tanner Andrews, Frank Ching, Stan Flewelling, Maryo and Zach Haag, Ellen Hale, Norigiku Horikawa, Lynne Horiuchi, Marcia Iwasaki, Lynn Larson, Jane Lundin, Barbara Masaki, Jack Natsuhara, Gail Nomura, John Pastier, Monica Sone, Tama Tokuda, Stephanie Toothman, Madeline Wilde, Eugenia Woo, and Sadie and Frank Yamasaki. Any remaining errors, of course, are the authors' responsibility entirely.

The staff at Manuscripts, Special Collections, and University Archives at the University of Washington Libraries deserve special mention since they have played a leading role in collecting material on Japanese American heritage. Sadie Yamasaki opened the Seattle Buddhist Temple Archives, which is an especially rich collection. The Seattle Public Schools Archives and Records Management Center, the collections of the Museum of History and Industry and the White River Valley Museum, and records held in the Washington State Archives also proved useful. In California, the Japanese American National Museum and the National Japanese American Historical Society provided access to their resources. Caroline Cole made it possible to include material from the collection of the Los Angeles Public Library. Rare materials in private collections were lent by Gerald Fukui, Takashi and Lily Hori, Henry Itoi, Jan Johnson, Alice M. Kawanishi, Kiyo Maekawa, Frank Natsuhara, Hiro Nishimura, Edward Sano and Monica Sone, among others. Considering the depth of losses sustained as a result of internment, I remain grateful for the gift of trust in lending family albums and other treasured possessions.

The project benefited from the generosity of a number of people who kindly arranged meetings, provided information or support, and helped in gaining access to the historic resources that are the subject of this work. They include James Arima, Rev. Don Castro, Gerald Fukui, Gerald Hedlund, Norigiku Horikawa, Eugene Itogawa, Jan Johnson, Tetsuden Kashima, Martha Makela, Nancy Shoji-Parent, Tim Schaefer, Cynthia Stroum, Linda Van Nest, Machiko Wada, Eugenia Woo and Karen Yoshitomi, to name but a few. Visits to several Seattle organizations generated useful information and a web of contacts, including the Japanese American Citizens League (Pacific Northwest District, Seattle and Lake Washington chapters), First Hill Lions Club, Nisei Veterans, Nikkei Concerns, the Seattle Buddhist Temple, and many others. Volunteer work at the beginning stages of the Densho Project proved important to my learning process.

Those who agreed to be interviewed deserve special acknowledgment, since their memories were the key to understanding Japanese American history from a personal perspective. Key informants were Frank Natsuhara, Kiyo Maekawa, Tom Matsuoka, Pedro and June Acosta, Elizabeth Slee and friends, Sam Shoji, Tama Tokuda, Edward Sano, Sue Kunitomi Embrey, and the many bowlers who willingly discussed the sport, including William Apao, Nobu Asami, Mark Fujimoto, Lon Honda and Fuzzy Shimada.

Personal thanks are due to Lisa Yost and Rachel Yost-Dubrow, for encouraging me in the work and accompanying me on the journey.

Donna Graves would like to acknowledge help in documenting Kuwabara Hospital/Midwifery from many people associated with San Jose's Japanese American Resource Center/Museum, including Ken Iwagaki, Jimi Yamaichi, George Yamaichi, Dr. Wright Kawakami, Lincoln Tokunaga, and Dr. Aggie Idemoto. Doris Otagaki graciously shared memories of her mother Mito Hori. Courtney Damkroger, San Jose's Historic Preservation Officer, shared information from the city's files. In Sebastopol, Reverend Carol J. Himaka shared important archival resources and arranged for Donna Graves' interviews with Enmanji Buddhist Temple elders Yoneko Shimizu and Minoru Matsuda. Jeannie Yang generously provided her research on the Temple. Research on the Holiday Bowl was enriched by conversations with Mitsue Kawaguchi, Joaquin Perez, Glen Kawaguchi, Duke Kim, Jack Tanaka, and Hatsuko Goto, who shared their own connections to the Bowl. Helen Liu Fong graciously offered her memories of designing the Sakiba.

Additionally, Eugenia Woo extends her gratitude to the LA Conservancy, Historic Resources Group, John English, Jack Laxer, and Eldon Davis/Victor Newlove. Karen Cheng thanks production assistants Jim Montgomery and Dan Hough, as well as Glenn Blue, owner of Olympus Press.

Names deserving of mention can inadvertently be overlooked in a project with an extended trajectory, so let me conclude with an expression of gratitude to all those who provided support and assistance. Thanks to you, the historic places in *Sento at Sixth and Main* will not soon be forgotten.